Be Brilliant at Behaviour Management

Practical behaviour strategies that work

Caroline Bentley-Davies

BLOOMSBURY EDUCATION
LONDON OXFORD NEW YORK NEW DELHI SYDNEY

BLOOMSBURY EDUCATION
Bloomsbury Publishing Plc
50 Bedford Square, London WC1B 3DP, UK
Bloomsbury Publishing Ireland Limited
29 Earlsfort Terrace, Dublin 2, D02 AY28, Ireland

BLOOMSBURY, BLOOMSBURY EDUCATION and the
Diana logo are trademarks of Bloomsbury Publishing Plc

First published in Great Britain, 2026 by Bloomsbury Publishing Plc

This edition published in Great Britain, 2026 by Bloomsbury Publishing Plc

Text copyright © Caroline Bentley-Davies, 2026

Image copyright (p21, 40, 90, 111–113) © Shutterstock
Image copyright (p5, 44) © Caroline Bentley-Davies, 2025

Caroline Bentley-Davies has asserted her right under the Copyright,
Designs and Patents Act, 1988, to be identified as Author of this work

Bloomsbury Publishing Plc does not have any control over, or responsibility for, any third-party websites referred to or in this book. All internet addresses given in this book were correct at the time of going to press. The author and publisher regret any inconvenience caused if addresses have changed or sites have ceased to exist, but can accept no responsibility for any such changes

All rights reserved. No part of this publication may be: i) reproduced or transmitted in any form, electronic or mechanical, including photocopying, recording or by means of any information storage or retrieval system without prior permission in writing from the publishers; or ii) used or reproduced in any way for the training, development or operation of artificial intelligence (AI) technologies, including generative AI technologies. The rights holders expressly reserve this publication from the text and data mining exception as per Article 4(3) of the Digital Single Market Directive (EU) 2019/790

A catalogue record for this book is available from the British Library

ISBN: PB: 978-1-8019-9767-6; eBook: 978-1-8019-9768-3

2 4 6 8 10 9 7 5 3 1 (paperback)

Cover design by Lauren Debono-Elliot

Typeset by Lumina Datamatics Ltd
Printed and bound in Great Britain by TJ Books, Padstow, Cornwall

To find out more about our authors and books visit www.bloomsbury.com
and sign up for our newsletters
For product safety-related questions contact productsafety@bloomsbury.com

Contents

Acknowledgements 4
About the author 5
Introduction: How to get the best out of this book 7

1 **What's your behaviour style?** A quick quiz 13

2 **Start right:** pre-empt problems and get into the right mindset 19

3 **Rules and routines:** because they matter 33

4 **I see you:** the importance of non-verbal communication 55

5 **The lesson:** managing behaviour through high expectations and quality teaching 73

6 **It's all about relationships** 89

7 **Voice control:** the importance of what you say and how you say it 105

8 **You are not alone:** engaging with others 127

Bibliography 139
Index 141

Acknowledgements

Special thanks for specific insights to: Edward Goodchild, Dr Daniel Coventry, Christopher Birks, Ross Bentley-Davies, Budge Bentley-Davies, and Teddy (my rescue foster dog). A huge thank you to the very talented Bloomsbury team for all their hard work and support. Thank you particularly to Joanna Ramsay, Kirsty Taylor, and Grace Kelly for their expertise, understanding and brilliant insights.

This book is for all the brilliant and hardworking teachers I've met over the years. Thank you for inviting me into your schools and into your lessons. And it's especially for those looking for solutions to manage behaviour better in their lessons.

About the author

Caroline Bentley-Davies has a wealth of expertise in behaviour management and trains teachers nationally and internationally. Not only does she observe lessons on a regular basis, she still teaches regularly too. She works with thousands of teachers and has over twenty years of experience teaching and working with schools and colleges. Caroline has multiple contracts to run Behaviour training events with ECTs, and school based teacher training institutes and universities. She has also seen an increasing demand for Behaviour Training for teachers across their teaching career in a whole school setting or via INSET training. Caroline is a trained coach and spends time each month helping teachers find strategies to improve their practice and enjoy becoming *Brilliant at Behaviour Management!*

Caroline has trained staff from over 150 schools and colleges in the last academic year, these have included primary schools, special schools, sixth form and further education colleges, state schools and independent schools.

Follow Caroline on X @realcbd, or Bluesky @realcbd.bsky.social.
For more details visit www.bentley-davies.co.uk.

Introduction

How to get the best out of this book

Welcome! I'm so pleased that you've chosen to read this book, and I'm looking forward to being your guide as we explore practical strategies to enable you to **'Be Brilliant at Behaviour Management.'**

This book has been in my mind for several years now. Every time I run training or receive feedback from teachers I get asked: *'Have you written a book on this topic, Caroline?'* or *'Where can I get all these great ideas in one place because my friend/neighbour/relative is a teacher and needs to know this too!'* Many teachers received scant behaviour management training when they first decided to be a teacher – and worryingly not much afterwards! Experienced teachers often tell me – it is so useful to receive updates, and they wish that they had known about some of these techniques before. There are already many great books on behaviour management out there but relatively few that are current and that cover *all* the challenges involved in managing behaviour supported by research and coaching too. This is where I come in!

Many of my training courses include a one-to-one coaching element and I have seen first-hand how coaching empowers and enthuses individual teachers, both newly qualified and experienced. Most importantly, a coaching approach ensures that any changes or new ideas that the teacher wants to adopt *do* actually happen. How often have you read a useful book or attended training and thought: *'Oh that's a great idea, I should try that out!'*– but then once the book closes or the session ends, you don't find time or can't commit to making those changes. All that great learning and momentum is then lost. My coaching approach helps cement the learning and will enable you to commit to making changes happen.

But *why* a coaching approach?

It's the most helpful way of encouraging *you* to make any changes to your management of behaviour and to make sure they stick. Coaching also depends on you as an individual to learn, decide and commit to clear actions and then review them, ultimately making the successful ones part of your regular toolkit of behaviour strategies. That is what makes this behaviour book so different to many others. But being great at managing pupil behaviour isn't just learning a repertoire of key techniques, however useful they may be. It depends on teachers applying what they've learnt to their individual circumstances and using their own judgement about their learners to decide which strategies *might* be best to help them resolve behaviour issues in lessons.

When we teach, we are dealing with large groups of learners with all their individual nuances, insecurities, complexities and varying needs. Each school or college is quite different, and to get the best out of managing behaviour each teacher needs to review which aspects of behaviour management they are most effective at and focus on improving the areas that could use some support.

Sometimes when we find managing behaviour tricky we can feel quite isolated. However, it might be reassuring to know that managing behaviour effectively is amongst the top three priorities of Senior Teachers in schools that I have visited recently. Although we might feel that we personally have behaviour 'sorted', a move to a different school, a promotion or a change within the school internally can really alter this. We can find ourselves trying to get established in a new and difficult terrain. It is important to know that over a teacher's whole professional life they will have all experienced challenging times. What makes the difference is those that seek to learn and become the best they can be – because there are strategies that work and skills we can develop to make things so much better for our pupils and ourselves.

How this book is structured

A lot of thought, planning and reviewing has gone into the contents of this book and it's ultimately a book for you to use in the way that best serves *your* needs. It's not a 'whodunnit' murder mystery novel, so if you decide that you simply *must* find out about the importance of 'non-verbal communication' or 'rules and routines', feel free to just select the chapters that are of particular interest and relevance to you. They work as stand-alone chapters packed full of useful tips, so you won't spoil any surprises if you don't read in chapter order! The book starts with a light-hearted (and illuminating) quiz which poses lots of thought-provoking questions about your individual reactions to behaviour. This will help direct you to the chapters of most use – ideal if you are short of time or just looking to hone your skills on a particular behaviour management aspect.

Likewise, you might have received feedback from a lesson observation indicating that areas of your teaching practice, such as student engagement, making transitions or giving instructions could benefit from targeted professional development. Therefore, you might decide to dip into the chapters relevant to improvement in those areas. Or perhaps you are the Head of Department or a mentor to a new teacher and can see that someone you are mentoring could use support and specific practical strategies. Steering them towards the specific chapters and talking through some of the strategies can be a supportive and time saving approach towards helping staff achieve better outcomes.

But of course, you can read the book right from Chapter 1 to the very end – and there's plenty of sense in doing it this way. You will receive a comprehensive compendium of useful behaviour management strategies, and you will be equipped for any behaviour eventuality – ideal if you are new to teaching or if you are looking to refresh your behaviour management tool kit.

At the end of the book there is a useful reading list and sign posting to other areas of support. The book is evidence and research based – but I've not clogged up each chapter with endless references which can be a barrier to an enjoyable reading experience.

Each chapter covers a main area of behaviour that we need to master to ensure the smooth running of a lesson – but importantly – we want the pupils in our care to enjoy learning and be more independent, self-motivated learners. Conducting lessons in absolute silence with draconian rules and harsh punishments might make for a peaceful lesson – but it doesn't meet our intentions. This guidance outlines how we can make our lessons engaging, interactive and worthwhile learning experiences whilst dealing with any behaviour issues that might crop up; and let's face it, when we want to arrange groupings or give detailed instructions, these are the times when things are likely to go askew! So, it's a book about enabling **Behaviour *for* Great Learning** and shares strategies that mean that we can make our lessons interactive and engaging without worrying about the behaviour.

Each chapter is structured using the classic coaching approach: **GROW**, which was popularised by Sir John Whitmore and Max Landsberg in 1992. You might already be familiar with this approach which helps individuals set and achieve meaningful goals (Whitmore, 1992). Essentially **GROW** takes us through practical steps towards making our goals a reality.

The GROW coaching approach explained

Goal

What is the desired end point? Goal looks at each specific area related to behaviour and paints a picture of what it would look like if this area was the *best* it could possibly be. It's important to start with the **Goal**, because this is what we are ultimately aiming for. Understanding what this looks like in detail is key. Although there will be some clear guidance and suggestions, the GOAL will be slightly different for everyone. A teacher looking at improving an aspect of their practice with an Early Years class will have different challenges and expectations to a PE teacher teaching a new sport to a GCSE class out on the field, for example. That is why there is an area for you to think about and refine your *own* goals.

Reality

What is the current situation in your classroom or education setting? What is working well and what could be improved? This section poses a number of thought-provoking questions and encourages you to make a note of your answers. For anything to improve there needs to be a **realistic assessment** of the current situation. What behaviour management strategies are working? What could be better? Where are the pain points (both for you and for your pupils)? Take time to ponder the questions posed as they will help you assess where you are.

Opportunities

This is where the real gold is! This longer section teaches you strategies to manage behaviour successfully – relating to the specific area of behaviour management that the chapter is based on. This is the most instructive part of the book with many teachable ideas and practical methods for you to take away and use. Within this section you will find **Interesting nuggets** and **Research nuggets**; key bite-sized facts and research relating to the chapter.

This section includes **Real-life cameos** which present examples connected to the chapter's main topic. These encourage you to reflect on a specific scenario in much more depth allowing you to understand the area in more detail. Some of these real-life cameos are straight from the classroom or real scenarios from a school or college. On occasion they are taken from a wider arena of life – showing how effective behaviour management can operate on a much larger scale.

Way forward

In the previous sections, you've thought about the **Goal**, reviewed the **Reality** of the situation and learned strategies for making improvement. You've been being given a selection of **Opportunities** to consider. The **Way forward** is where you reflect on what you've learnt and are encouraged to make a choice about actioning a few suggested ideas as your Way forward. I encourage you to note these down as your planned approach so that you really think about what it will look like to take these precise steps. You can use the **Way forward** part of the book – or if the book is not your own copy then in a notebook or electronic device – to jot your intentions down. Planning a few key changes really makes the difference. It's important not to try and undertake too many changes at once because that can be overwhelming – but a commitment to a few key areas will be a real game changer.

I delivered some training at a school in Greater Manchester for groups of teachers who were looking to upskill in Behaviour Management. Although they absorbed, got involved with and enjoyed the initial training, what really made a difference was each of them selecting a few key things to work on. They made a commitment to try out these techniques over a set period with targeted classes. We met again six weeks later for further training and feedback on the impact of the strategies. They all felt that making a commitment to undertaking some clear actions had a noticeable impact of improving behaviour and the learning climate in their lessons. One Technology teacher said that he could hardly believe the difference in not only his pupils' behaviour – but also in his improved relationship with them. The commitment and persistence to try a limited number of critical things in a focused way really helped to transform the behaviour in his lessons.

So, let's get started! Complete the questionnaire in the next chapter and give honest responses to the scenarios. This will help set the scene and give you some direction to the chapters that will help you most. If you're already clear about which chapters you want to read first – dive in!

I'd love to hear how you are getting on with the book and any thoughts or questions you have – so feel free to drop me a line either through my website listed below (where you can find out about training opportunities too), or join my community on X @realcbd, Bluesky @realcbd.bsy.social or LinkedIn.

Warmest wishes,
Caroline Bentley-Davies
www.bentley-davies.co.uk

1 What's your behaviour style? A quick quiz

The following light-hearted questionnaire is designed to help you reflect upon your main approaches to behavioural issues in lessons. For each question, think about the situation and choose the answer that best suits. There might be more than one answer that applies to you, but as I say to a pupil who is reluctant to answer – which one would you pick – if you could receive £50 for your answer?! 'I don't have £50 available,' as I always say – but it does focus the mind, and they always give me an answer.

1. **In your opinion, the teacher's essential tool in managing behaviour successfully is their…**
    a. Lesson plan (a great lesson plan is critical!). The lesson is planned to ensure great learning – but also with thoughts as to how to create a smooth, well-managed lesson with good behaviour. For example: thinking about the timings of activities, and pre-planning how to deal with aspects pupils might find challenging. This heads off tricky behaviour.
    b. Ability to create rapport and connect with their students. Relationships are fundamental.
    c. Rules and sanctions. Having lots of clear rules and reinforcing them through sanctions. Be clear and always following through on them.
    d. The ability to call for support or 'back up' from senior staff.
    e. Non-verbal communication cues. Pupils pick up very quickly whether you mean business by how you move and act!

2. **It's well into mid-term, and things are feeling a bit tough with your class. You decide that behaviour is best reset by…**
    a. Re-organising the seating plan. Nothing says a reset like showing them you are changing things and breaking up unhelpful clusters of chatty pupils.
    b. A team talk. Telling your class that you feel 'disappointed' in them and that you expect better will hopefully motivate them and do the trick.
    c. Getting tough! Clamping down on any infractions of the rules. This will remind them that you are in charge.

d. Getting the Senior Leadership Team (SLT) or Head of Department involved. They can decide what will happen if this poor behaviour continues.

   e. Increasing the praise and using the reward system when pupils are doing things right. Being aware of your facial expressions and being very effective scanning the room – so you can reset positive behaviour and 'pre-empt' those about to go off task.

3 **After a difficult lesson you are most likely to have lost your…**

   a. Resources. Your heart sinks when you see the cards etc. scattered around the room. You spent so long making them.

   b. Self-esteem. It feels very personal when pupils don't do what they should.

   c. Lunch break and free time. Many detentions will have been set or minutes of break time lost.

   d. Next free lesson. You've spent it explaining to the SLT why so many students have been removed from your class.

   e. Composure. Normally you are like a swan: sailing smoothly above water, with your feet paddling furiously underneath. But in this lesson, you feel your usual calm approach slipping.

4 **After a term being taught by you – you'd most like your pupils to be impressed by your…**

   a. Ability to plan engaging and interesting lessons.

   b. Caring approach – knowing them all well as individuals.

   c. Firm nature and ability to maintain silence in the room.

   d. Contacts in the SLT and ability to escalate the situation.

   e. Ability to scan the room quickly to find out who isn't on task. And the ability to predict who is just about to try and eat something.

5 **You think body language and non-verbal communication is…**

   a. Something you really hadn't considered.

   b. A way of showing you care – smiling and eye contact, for example.

   c. Less important than what you say.

   d. Something you've noticed that the SLT really have mastered.

   e. A crucial part of your behaviour management technique.

6 **The animal that best represents your approach to behaviour is…**

   a. A horse – functional, multi-talented and hardworking.

   b. A pet rabbit – fluffy, kind and reassuring.

c. A lion – the boss, regal and powerful.

   d. A cat – it's the symbol of the House you are in. And you need to stay 'on school message'.

   e. A sheep dog – you are often herding and managing the group (though honestly, sometimes you feel a little like a sheep!).

7. **Your pet peeve with low level poor behaviour is…**

   a. Pupils who roll up or draw on resources that you have taken hours to create.

   b. Pupils who say things meaning to be hurtful to you, such as: 'I hate French…' or 'I preferred my teacher last year. He was much better than you!'

   c. Pupils who try to argue with you when they have clearly been caught breaking the rules.

   d. Pupils repeatedly talking and being silly. But then behaving like angels when SLT walk in the room.

   e. Pupils not having the correct resources with them.

8. **When your class is too noisy and you want to get their attention you…**

   a. Move to the place in the classroom where you always issue instructions. Pupils soon stop talking as they know you will be telling them what is next.

   b. Tell them to 'shhh!'

   c. Shout.

   d. Try everything you can think of – bells, signals – you've tried them all.

   e. Use a non-verbal sign – such as a hand gesture, or another approach to draw them in.

9. **You feel that asking for help or telling others about challenges you are having with a class or individual pupil is…**

   a. A useful way of finding out if other people have strategies that might be helpful and a way of sharing information.

   b. A problem shared is a problem halved. You are keen to share and hear from others too.

   c. A sign of weakness. You keep any problems to yourself.

   d. A frequent occurrence – but you'd like some help getting resolutions.

   e. You prefer to seek advice by watching and observing someone else – you find this more effective – than talking through ideas.

10 **One of the things that you think people underestimate in regard to managing behaviour in lessons…**
   a. How tiring it is to both teach content and manage behaviour.
   b. The emotional toll of battling difficult behaviour.
   c. How some people find it easier than others.
   d. How little time is spent during teacher training sessions learning how to manage behaviour, with greater emphasis placed on curriculum content and learning theory.
   e. How past experiences and knowledge from other jobs and roles can help diffuse conflict.

11 **On recent behaviour training you heard discussions about how some pupils are 'Alphas and influencers' whose behaviours and attitudes can sway the class negatively or positively and you thought…**
   a. Yep, it's true that when some pupils are absent behaviour is better.
   b. You wish you'd known before – you'd like to know how to influence these pupils better.
   c. You are the only Alpha in the room!
   d. You actually see it in the staff room on training – some groups sway the response of the whole school at Inset training – often the PE department! You've always thought the SLT were in charge of Inset, but you can see that there are groups that influence things – negatively or positively. How can you use this information in your lessons?
   e. You are aware that some learners adopt these roles, and that it is important to be aware of – but also you need to include and engage these key elements – so their influence can be harnessed for the benefit of all the class.

Identify which letter appears most frequently across your answers. The answer options for each question broadly relate to the five following approaches to dealing with difficult behaviour in lessons as a class teacher. It is expected that you will have a range of different letters represented, but which is the most common?

If you have selected mainly (a) your colour is:

A – Blue: Chapters 3 and 7

You have a sensible approach towards managing pupil behaviour. Your actions are focused on the areas that you can control, such as planning engaging lessons and managing the physical layout of the classroom. It's likely that you are methodical and generally well organised. You tend to follow school systems. You are right to think carefully about your lesson planning and how best to capture the interest of pupils – because getting pupils engaged and interested is important in directing them away from the opportunities for poor behaviour that can happen when they get bored or distracted. There are lots more tools in the behaviour toolkit that will help you conserve your energy, and these are important to use in conjunction with great planning. Start with Chapter 3 and Chapter 7 for alternative strategies that you can add to your repertoire to improve behaviour.

If you have selected mainly (b) your colour is:

B – Orange: Chapters 2 and 5

You really care about the pupils you teach, and you are correct – good relationships are the bedrock of great behaviour. When you make the effort to really know pupils as individuals, and help them overcome their challenges, behaviour improves. Pupils need to know that we care, and one way of doing this is to have a calm lesson with high standards of behaviour. It is great to be a teacher who has empathy with pupils, but we also have to make sure that we don't dip into having too much sympathy – as this can sometimes lead to excusing aspects of behaviour. Keep that warm nature, but also look at Chapter 2 and Chapter 5 which offer tips and techniques to add to your approach. These will be particularly useful when encountering new classes or unknown individuals where you can't rely on relationships that have already been built.

If you have selected mainly (c) your colour is:

C – Red: Chapters 5 and 6

You are the boss of the classroom, and you have a clear list of rules and regulations. Woe betide anyone who thinks that they can pull the wool over your eyes. You are not slow at handing out sanctions. And you might even have the record of the person who has issued most detentions last year! It is clear that the teacher must be the person in charge of the room. And it's also important to make sure that your strong authority doesn't inflame situations and that it doesn't create an adversarial approach in the lessons. Of course, it is important to uphold the school rules and systems. Being consistent is one of your strengths. However, if pupils feel that ultimately you are not on their side then they will resist your lessons. Make sure you look at how you can add warmth and influence to managing behaviour so that it is not just a battle of wills. To help you add to your repertoire perhaps look at Chapters 5 and 6.

If you have selected mainly (d) your colour is:

D – Yellow: Chapters 2 and 4

You are very keen to do the correct thing about behaviour. You are also a person who carefully follows the school sanction systems. You sometimes feel a little out of your depth with behaviour and one of your main approaches is to rely on the support of the SLT when things become tricky. You are absolutely right to use the school systems. It is perfectly appropriate to use the 'call back-up' approach, and supporting colleagues is a key role of the SLT. If your school offers detentions centrally then using them seems very sensible. However, it is important to keep building and developing your own behavioural management skills too. Use the systems that there are – but make sure that you are putting into play all the ways you can to develop your own behaviour management skills. Have a look at Chapters 2 and 4 to help you build your confidence and hone that expertise.

If you have selected mainly (e) your colour is:

E – Purple: Chapters 3 and 5

You take a thoughtful approach to behaviour management, and you draw upon a whole wealth of knowledge. You are skilled at influencing pupils and in predicting behaviour. You make good use of your presence and your non-verbal skills to manage behaviour successfully. These aren't skills that all teachers are obviously aware of, so you have lots to offer. There are, of course, many other strategies and approaches that are successful too, and you might find it useful to start by looking at Chapters 3 and 5 to see other ways of adding to your skills.

2 Start right: pre-empt problems and get into the right mindset

Each essential area for being brilliant at behaviour management will be considered in detail in its own chapter. But it is often the case that I'm asked for general advice for dealing with a new class and making the right first impression. With this in mind, this chapter looks at how to 'start right' and pre-empt difficult behaviours before they begin. It might be the case that you want to 'start right' with new classes in September, or maybe you are a trainee teacher looking for strategies for taking over a class as part of your teaching practice. It could be that you are wanting to have a 'reset' and a fresh start with some classes as an experienced teacher. Whatever your reason, the strategies in this chapter will help you maximise these crucial first impressions.

Goal: creating strong lesson foundations

Whilst the beginning of a new term or fresh school year is exciting, the reality of teaching a new class, or starting at a new school or college can actually be quite daunting. There is a golden window of opportunity to get things right. When we start well, we are setting up rules and routines that will serve us for the rest of the year. We want a smooth running to our lessons. We don't want to battle for good behaviour. We want to set things up securely so that we can focus on learning, rather than fire-fighting difficult or obstructive behaviour. The start we make matters.

Why do first impressions matter so much?

Our goal is to create a good first impression with our learners so that they quickly realise that we are a strong, effective teacher who is deserving of their respect, attention and compliance. The aim is to create an atmosphere in lessons of hard work, positivity and 'flow' where pupils feel proud of the learning that they have achieved. We want the pupils to see this as a partnership between us as the teacher and them as a learner. Our goal is to have strong enough behaviour management strategies so that we can create interesting and engaging lessons. Just like riding a horse, we shouldn't keep the reins taught and tense. We want to be able to loosen them to allow the horse independence to choose their route through rocky terrain, confident that we can signal and pull them back on course when necessary. In the case of our pupils and classroom environments, we want to allow dialogue, group work and autonomy. Pupils should feel confident enough in our relationship and classroom routines that we can quickly signal and pull them back to the lesson focus when necessary.

We know that there will be challenges and difficult situations in lessons – whether it's the wasp that flies through the classroom window or a more serious issue brewing. You might be dealing with a class that comes in with a bad attitude because they have been told off in a previous lesson, or they're still 'high energy' after a behaviour incident at lunch. Whatever it is, we want to have put in the groundwork so that we can manage the situations that crop up with the least amount of disruption possible. This will help us to get back to the main priority: good teaching and learning in a safe, happy and controlled environment.

Research nugget

Mihaly Csikszentmihalyi derived the concept of 'flow' which is the state of concentration and engagement that happens when one is immersed in a task that is appropriately challenging and absorbing (Csikszentmihalyi, 1975). You know it's happened when pupils feel that the lesson has flown by so quickly – because they have been so absorbed. This is what we are aiming for, at least in some of the lesson. It involves complete concentration and absorption with the learning in hand.

Reality: get set!

When sprinters race, they start at different positions on a racetrack. It first appears that the runners on the outside lanes will need to cover a greater distance. However, to ensure that the race is fair, runners are given a staggered start – those runners on the outside track begin further ahead than the others on the inside track. This ensures that everyone runs *exactly* the same distance even though they are starting in different positions on the track.

Figure 1: Runners at staggered points on a race track.

Think about where you are starting on this track. Do you feel ahead of the race right from the start? Have you thought carefully about how you can make a strong start? Are you aware of what you can do to make a good start or are you likely to 'wing' it' and make mistakes and false starts? Do you know what you can do to get ahead and instil calm authority with the class? Do you have a range of strategies? If you've not given this area much thought before then fear not, we will unpack a toolkit of ideas to help you make the very best start possible.

Opportunities: focusing your energy where impact is possible

There are some things that, of course, are beyond your direct control, like what has happened to the student before they arrive at your lesson, or what their home-life is like. This information is of critical importance and it is vital that pastoral teams have accurate and up-to-date knowledge, so that they can take any actions necessary. But in the throes of a busy lesson, it is important to focus on the areas that are directly *within* your control. There are also areas that you might not have the direct ability to control but that you can influence. These are also critical in managing behaviour effectively.

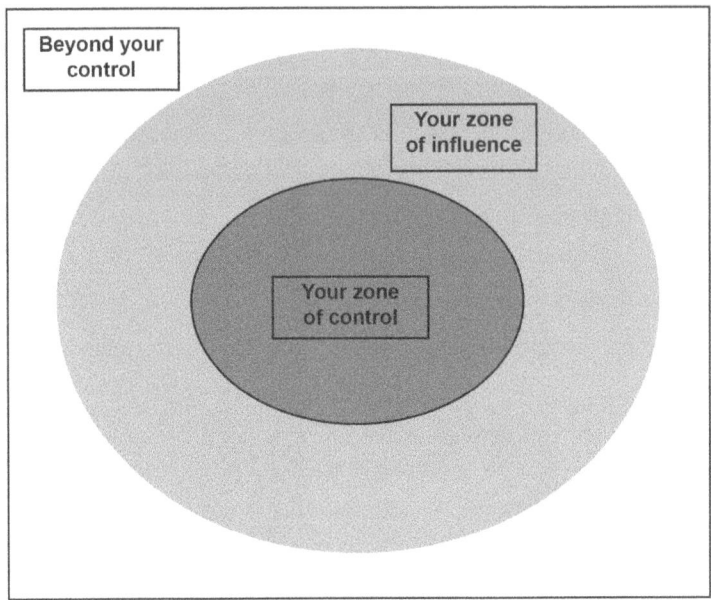

Figure 2: Zones of control and influence

Figure 2 shows a useful diagram to explain this. There are a range of things that you can directly control – for example, creating an effective lesson plan and having everything prepped before you start and how you speak and react to the students. Bear in mind this area is not huge, however, there are a greater number of aspects that you can *influence*, even if you can't *directly* control them. This is helpful because you realise that there is a lot you can do to help make the lesson run more smoothly, for example providing strategies to assist students who might get stuck, or thinking about how you group the students so that they are more likely to work harmoniously with each other. Outside the zone of influence are all the aspects that are *beyond* your control, for example, a pupil's home life or the pupils' previous negative experiences or assumptions they may have about the topic that you are teaching. The key is to look at the areas that we *can* control and to think carefully how to best leverage your zone of influence.

Priming the Environment

Setting up the space or classroom (priming) that you are teaching in is very useful in influencing behaviour. We see evidence of priming all around us, whether it is in the supermarket, train station or many other places in modern society.

Research nugget

Researchers investigated whether the music playing influenced shopper choice of wine in a supermarket. They found that when French music was played shoppers bought significantly more French wine, and when German music was played more German wine was sold. But when shoppers were asked whether the music had influenced their choice, the majority said it hadn't. Of course, wine has no place in lessons, but the example does show how people's behaviour can be influenced by their settings and surroundings – in this case through the music they were hearing (Hargreaves and McKendrick, 1999).

A teacher friend of mine plays very soothing instrumental music during parts of her maths lesson whilst the class are independently problem solving. She feels that it helps them calmly look at the problems for a specified amount of time. Importantly, she uses it a cue. While the music is playing, they understand that they need to be working through the problems on their own, and when it stops, they will discuss them as a class. It should be said, though I've not been able to find research evidence to actually prove its effectiveness – it definitely seemed to help her set up a routine and helps cue in the class to the fact that they should be working independently. We might not choose to use music in our lessons – but there are other effective ways we can prime behaviour.

Priming strategies are designed to influence our actions – and we can also positively influence our students into making good choices regarding their behaviour and attitudes to learning.

If you've ever been trying to eat more healthily and have walked into a staff room that has a plate of tempting cakes just sitting there, then you will know how hard it is to resist, particularly if you have to go right past. It takes active effort to say 'no'. If we are trying to adopt healthy eating habits at home, we can consciously prime our environment to help us make better choices. For example, by having a bowl of easy-to-peel fruit in handy reach or keeping treats in a cupboard, out of sight, making it much easier to make healthier choices.

Strategies for priming the environment

What can we do to 'prime' the environment for our pupils so that they are more likely to behave? Think about how the environment first appears to them. How can it be planned better? Think about:

- **Seating:** Are students more likely to look at you and the board than each other? How can you arrange the seating to influence this?
- **The view:** When setting up a new space, try and sit in each desk or space – can you see the board clearly? Does the light shine on the screen? Are there any 'hidden or blind spot areas' where pupils might be able to 'hide' from you? If you are teaching Reception pupils – what is at their eye level? How is it if you are sat on the carpet? What can you see?
- **Grouping:** Who are they sat next to? Do you decide or do you let them sit with their friends where they might be more prone to chat and get distracted? By organising the seating as the teacher, you are also demonstrating ownership of the space. This shows that you are the boss and sets the correct tone. You can also make sure that any pupils' needs are appropriately catered for, such as having students who are hard of hearing or partially sighted in the best location to access the lesson.
- **Solving common issues:** You can also pre-empt common issues like dealing with lateness, by having a table at the front on the side so that any late comers can sit there without disrupting the rest of the class. It also means you can easily have a quiet word to find out the reason for their tardiness once they are settled without having to conduct this conversation across the room.
- **Using displays:** How can you make displays work for you to reinforce great expectations and showcase quality learning? Highlighting pupils' work on display where they have made a real effort is one way. Using displays interactively to provide support and as starting places for pupils who get 'stuck' to help get themselves 'unstuck' is also a helpful way of setting high expectations and giving pupils a resource to learn from.
- **Setting behaviour standards:** Use the 'ripple effect' from one class to the next to influence pupils to behave effectively. For example, making sure that the class leaving the lesson exit in an organised, calm and collected way – rather than like a noisy rabble. If you dismiss the class in stages in a sedate manner – it will also set a calm atmosphere for those who are about to enter the room. You have set the standard about suitable behaviour that is expected for your class.

- **Effective and efficient systems:** To deal with things that might distract from pupils getting on with their learning. For example: providing pens and equipment that can be easily accessed, rather than students using this as an excuse to distract and cause off-task behaviour. It is worth thinking about what items, resources or queries are likely to derail a lesson and to think ahead about how to prevent this.
- **Visual appeal:** A place that looks cared for is much more likely to create better behaviour. I know that if I let a class leave when there's some debris and a mess, even just a few scrunched up bits of paper on the desk or leftover resources, then the next class will leave even more behind and behaviour, efforts and standards will slide.

People automatically look for cues on how to behave and treat their environment based on the behaviour of others around them. You might have seen this in meetings or training sessions – one person checks their phone and suddenly lots of people are engaging in distracted behaviours. After fifteen minutes, half of the room are engaging in other activities – however subtly. You may also feel awkward about being the *first* one to check your phone and send texts if other people haven't already started. In fact, people go to great efforts not to be the one who initiates that first 'off task step'. We take our cues about how to behave and what is acceptable by quickly noting (sometimes subconsciously) what is the norm (and therefore considered acceptable) behaviour around us. Our class will soon realise what is permitted and non-permitted behaviour. Let's prime the environment to set those high expectations and then follow through with our actions.

> ### Research nugget
>
> The research regarding litter dropping in public showed that the amount of rubbish on the ground increased in direct proportion to the amount of rubbish that was there already. For example, when researchers added more rubbish to the ground, increasing it from one, two, four and eight pieces, the percentage of people who dropped rubbish increased from 10, 20, 23 and 41 per cent respectively. As there was already evidence that rubbish on the ground was 'normal behaviour' people followed this behavioural trend. They dropped their litter and took less care. But when there was less litter, people followed accordingly and did not leave their rubbish on the ground (Cialdini, Reno and Kallgren, 1990).

If, in our actions and comments as a teacher, we direct students towards the social norm of behaving in a particular way, then they are much more likely to follow. For example, when briefing about homework at the start of the year, set the clear expectation that all students must complete their homework on time. Let students know that last year every student completed the homework on time and it was not necessary to set any detentions for late homework. Explain clearly what students should do if they get 'stuck' with a piece of work and ensure that you give sufficient time to complete it. It is important to set these behavioural norms early so that the good behaviour is observed by all. It is then much easier to embed good habits.

I see you…

We are all animals and have been programmed to quickly read situations and to size up others – particularly strangers. We are deciding if they pose threats, or whether they are potential foes or allies. This is hardwired into us because in the ancient past our very survival depended on our ability to make quick decisions about the intentions of others.

Your pupils will be weighing you up very carefully and deciding what they think you will be like as a teacher. Will you be a teacher who accepts late homework and a less than stellar effort? Or will you be a teacher who really strives and works alongside them to help achieve their best? Are you a teacher who loves teaching and is looking forward to developing their skills?

You might already also have a school 'reputation', or they might have heard something about you from a sibling/friend, and whether this is true or not, it will set their expectations. They might also have false and/or stereotypical assumptions about you because of your experience. Perhaps you look very young and they might erroneously think this will make you less effective or that they can misbehave and get away with it! We can't easily control our pupils' assumptions, but we can challenge and correct them through our actions. The first impressions we give with a class sets the tone for future interactions. This is why it is important to have positive but firm early interactions with *all* pupils in the class to disrupt any false ideas that they might have and to signal that you will be teaching and managing behaviour successfully.

Be transparent about your rules, routines and consequences. Pupils are often looking to spot unfairness and contradiction, and can easily recognise who doesn't follow through on what they say they will. Make sure you are clear on the school behaviour and sanctions system ahead of lessons and seek clarification on any aspects that you are unsure about.

Most importantly, pupils are looking for an enthusiastic, expert teacher who enjoys interacting with pupils. Thinking hard about how to create this impression is important. Don't try to be someone else. Instead, be the best version of yourself. This is helped by:

Priming yourself

It is impossible and undesirable to script everything you want to say to the class. Pupils respond best to a dynamic, interactive teacher who responds 'in the moment'. However, there is a time when it can be useful to script a few things. These include the very first words you might say with your new class, some key instructions and potentially some 'mini scripts' to deal with the most likely things to go askew in those first few lessons. Even if you don't use these scripted sayings, your confidence will benefit from having thought about different scenarios. You will also have the opportunity to choose *how* to present yourself and to ensure that you are showing your positive side, demonstrating competence, warmth and confidence. This is important for influencing how the class will respond to you.

Real life cameo: scripting your lesson start

When I'm running a high stakes demonstration lesson or giving an important workshop, I will often have scripted my opening sentence. I will have it written down but, once I start, I don't actually tend to look at it. Knowing it's there bolsters my confidence and if I'm having an 'off day', I can use it to guide me. I don't have to hum and haw and look awkward and lacking in confidence in front of a class and observers. I really recommend that others do this, particularly when you are getting started with a new class. It takes seconds – but makes for a much better start. Don't forget to include the positives too.

For example: *'Great to meet you, Year 9 – you are in for a treat with Art this year. We are going to be doing some really interesting projects. I'm Miss Jones and I'm just going to run through the three main rules of my Art room – so listen up…'*

Professional sports people often run through sequences in their head visualising success. Professional golfers, for example, imagine themselves taking a difficult shot and see themselves in slow motion running through the actions to a successful conclusion. It is a good idea to visualise your intentions ahead of your very first key lesson. Ask yourself:

- How do you imagine looking?
- How will you be standing?
- What is your posture like?
- How will you greet pupils as they arrive?

If you can see yourself teaching an accomplished lesson in your mind's eye it will build your confidence. Think about what message is being transmitted through your posture and the words you choose and imagine the pupils' response. Think about the clarity of the instructions that you are about to give. You might want to record these on your planning sheet, so you feel confident that they are there if you need them.

Real life cameo: anticipating obstacles through visualisation

On one occasion I was teaching an important transition lesson and I wanted it to go really well. As I was planning it, I visualised it running in a sped up version in my head – like a fast forward film. As I did so, I realised that not only were my instructions for an important part the task unclear but I had forgotten to get a key resource ready which was needed in the second half of the lesson. Spending a few minutes running through the sequence of the lesson in my mind enabled me to see where it might have gone wrong. I was able to make amendments both to my instructions and I made sure that I had the necessary equipment ready. When I actually came to teach the lesson it was a real success! Spending just a few minutes previewing the lesson in my mind's eye really helped.

Preparing yourself…

Think about what *you* might respond with if your pupils say:

- I'm stuck…
- I don't understand… (before having a try themselves)
- I hated science last year!
- But they're also eating…
- Can I go to the toilet?
- That's not fair!
- Other pupils say you are too soft…too strict…too…
- Are you a new teacher?
- How old are you?
- We did this last year...
- It's too hard/too easy/too different

If you're an experienced teacher, I'm sure you have many more things you can add to that list. And even though you might not use them, and of course, you have to be flexible, having pre-planned responses can be so useful. However, don't say phrases in a way that sounds like you are reciting the information. It needs to sound natural and responsive – even if it is pre-planned. Many of the pre-planned responses could be used in different circumstances.

Imagine the following situation: you 'catch' a student eating and you tell them to put their sweets or crisps away as your first response. This is quite a moderate response, and you are giving them the opportunity to get back on track. But when they don't, you give a staged warning or demerit (or whatever is the school consequence system). You do this in a logical way, verbalising your reasoning: *'I've already asked you to put away your sweets, Jothen.'* Pause to give the student another opportunity to do the right thing. Continue with: *'And you haven't. So now you need to give them to me…'* The student gets hot and bothered and tries to argue and bluff his way out of it by claiming that there were other pupils, Ben and Jamil, who were also eating. He tries to get you to punish them too or let him off because of this perceived unfairness. He gives you the sweets, but it's clear that he wants to make a big thing about it. You had no idea that there were other pupils possibly breaking this rule. There is the chance here that the lesson might become totally derailed as a result of Jothen undermining your request. You need to retain control and bring the focus back to the work quickly. Fortunately, you have already thought about what to say if you are accused of not treating pupils fairly, or when pupils argue with the clear rules. So, you are able to calmly say what you have pre-planned for this eventuality:

> 'That **might** be the case Jothen – but it was **you** I saw eating just now. You need to concentrate on **your** behaviour. If I see **anybody** else eating, then the same consequence will apply to them. Now, let's get on with looking at the extract… Who can tell me why the writer…'

You have already decided that you will react calmly and logically. You successfully re-focus Jothen and encourage him to think about his own behaviour whilst also sending a clear message to the class that you will not accept anyone else breaking this rule. Of course, if you find yourself using this example frequently then you might want to practise scanning the room more frequently to make sure your students are adhering to your rules!

Having your pre-planned responses will make things a lot smoother and gets you in the right mindset. It also helps you regulate your own emotions, as you can practise key statements beforehand by saying them out loud, which can help prevent poor behaviour from escalating.

The words you use matter

Think about how you will use language to inspire and get pupils on side. Think about building a class team spirit right from the start. You are the leader of the class and you need your pupils to 'buy into' your leadership. Using words such as 'we' and 'us' rather than 'you' gives the impression that you are all working together towards a common goal and as such, it creates rapport with the class which can be very motivating.

Imagine you have marked a set of assessments and the class have not done very well. It seems clear to you that they have not put in enough effort. Imagine how they might feel if you tell them: *'Well class, the assessments weren't very good – at all! You are all going to have to work much harder'*. Then flip this phrasing slightly: *'Well class, the assessments didn't show your full potential. We are all going to have to work much harder.'* Although the second example still suggests that the class are going to have to work harder, by including the word, *'we'*, the teacher shows the class that they are all 'in it together' and they will work hard with their class to help improvements happen. It's a small change of words – but it makes a big difference to motivation and behaviour.

Remember that all of these examples need to feel natural to you. So thinking, pre-planning and rehearsing the phrases that you might choose to use is key.

Way forward

After reading this chapter, you will have some helpful strategies to add to your toolkit for starting out with a class effectively or starting afresh with your current class. It is worth thinking about:

- How you want to be perceived.
- What pre-planning and preparation you can do to make a good start.
- What specific aspects of starting right will be most important in your context.

Take a moment to reflect on how you can 'start right'. Think about where things are going well for you, and what might be areas for development. Let's first look to the positives.

Skills that I think I have mastered already in this area:

_____

_____

_____

_____

_____

_____

_____

I would like to reflect on these aspects of 'starting well':

1 _____

2 _____

3 _____

The planned actions I am going to take are:

1 _____

2 _____

3 _____

Review: How did it go? What did I learn? What are my reflections? When I have a 'new' start in the future, what will I keep and what might I change?

_____
_____
_____
_____
_____
_____
_____
_____
_____
_____
_____
_____
_____
_____
_____
_____
_____
_____
_____
_____

3 Rules and routines: because they matter

Are you a rule maker or a rule breaker? Some teachers are sticklers for all rules and enforce them rigidly. Other teachers have themselves been rule breakers in the past and therefore struggle with consistency in setting rules and holding their pupils accountable. They sometimes just 'hope for the best'. However, rules are connected with routines, procedures and relationships. They are also an essential part of the preventive layer of behaviour management and, as such, deserve exploring.

Goal: establishing rules and routines

Think for a moment about a fantastically run lesson where all pupils are learning well and are cooperating with you and each other. Are you actually aware of the existence of rules? From my experience of observing thousands of lessons, rules mainly tend to be mentioned with persistence when they are *not* being followed. When a lesson is running smoothly, the rules are so well established they seem almost non-existent – but they are definitely still there. Pupils have a firm and clear understanding and follow the (well established) rules without being constantly reminded. The rules are like an invisible barrier to prevent poor behaviour. If it appears that a rule *might* be broken, then a brief glance or perhaps stepping a little closer to where the potential rule breaker is sitting will bring them back on task without a public, and potentially embarrassing reprimand. This is one reason why rules really matter. They set a clear line of permitted behaviour and pupils know where they stand.

Consistent rules for all learners

Many pupils, especially those with ADHD, prefer clear boundaries and rules. They want to know exactly what is and isn't allowed. These students, like most others, are acutely sensitive to fairness and injustices real or perceived. They often want to be treated scrupulously fairly. Rules that are opaque or punishments issued seemingly on a whim can really cause the relationship between teachers and pupils to break down.

This is generally the case more widely, outside the classroom too. I experienced this myself when tried to check in to a fancy hotel for my birthday trip an hour early, as the traffic had been favourable. The guidelines were clearly signposted on the booking: *'check in from 4pm'*. I hopefully suggested to the receptionist that although it was only 3pm, perhaps my room might be ready? Could they please just check? The receptionist looked furtively around reception and then agreed to let me in earlier. I thought it was my charm that had persuaded him, but he admitted that he only felt he could let me in early because there were no other customers in reception also wanting to check in early. *'People kick off,'* he confided in me, *'If they feel that they are not having the same rules applied to them.'* Fairness, or the appearance of fairness is key, it appears in the smooth running of everyday life, not just the classroom!

Of course, there will be times when you'll need to set or adjust the rules explicitly. This is especially the case when they relate to a very specific situation such as using a piece of new equipment in design and technology, or taking part in something highly dangerous, like javelin, or when briefing specific expectations for a school trip. For the most part, the goal of having rules is that they form part of the unwritten support system of the classroom that everybody knows is there with little need to mention them, once they've been firmly established.

Real life cameo: classroom code

A very successful teacher I know told me that she views rules in a lesson the same as the 'rules of the road' when driving. She explains that all drivers know these motoring laws as set out in the Highway Code, and the same can be said for her classroom rules. *'My class know that certain things are always prohibited, like eating in class or playing with their mobile phones.'* Pupils are not permitted to randomly move or get out of their seats during lessons. Of course, there are a myriad of other smaller regulations and procedures for the smooth running of the lesson too. *'I establish these rules early on with my class. They know, like when driving, some behaviours such as using a mobile phone are always strictly prohibited. However, when driving, different areas require different speed limits, so the rules change. Likewise, my general class rules are firmly established but when we change*

> *activity within a lesson, perhaps from taking a test which demands silent, individual concentration, to taking part in group work, which allows some active participation and consultation with others, I remind them of the rules connected with the new task: in this case, successful group working. For example, for group work to be successful discussion relating to the task is allowed. One person per group is also usually allocated to retrieve the equipment from the storage area, allowing these pupils to leave their seats. I usually briefly remind them of these procedures to ensure the smooth running of the next "group work" part of the lesson. But I give these rule reminders just before the specific change of task, so pupils are not overloaded with too many contradicting rules.'*

Clear classroom routines that reinforce your rules

Setting up routines is the best way to support your rules, and well managed routines can help a classroom run like clockwork. The history of the word 'routine' comes from 1670s Old French and refers to a road, or route. In the same way establishing a regular routine can be a roadmap to a calm and purposeful lesson. The best routine, like the best road, is only effective once it is well established. When a road is first created it is perhaps just a track made by animals or people repeatedly walking a certain direction. Its surface is uneven and there might be rocks or other dangerous or unwelcome debris strewn across the path hindering travellers' progress. For the road to become truly effective it needs to become established and well maintained.

This applies to classroom routines too. For routines to become well established and maintained, they need to be clearly thought out by the teacher *before* the lesson and persistently reinforced *during* the lesson. Pupils might need frequent verbal reminders. It is only when the routines become clear, and the teacher perseveres with them, that they become firmly embedded into regular practice and are therefore useful. The path to good behaviour is much easier to tread.

There are some clear times where **great routines** really help us establish our goal of great behaviour management. If you are an experienced teacher you are likely to have some tried and tested routines that really work for you. But it is also worth asking yourself: are there parts of my lesson that might benefit from improved routines?

These include the **starts of lessons** which are absolutely critical because they set the tone. I observe hundreds of lessons a year, and I've witnessed first-hand how an organised, positive start is instrumental for smooth and successful learning.

In the same way, managing the starts of different activities *within* the lesson allows for an organised classroom atmosphere. Managing transitions well is vital because changes in activity, tempo or group organisation can create moments of disruption to the lesson flow. There is potential for pupils to become 'lost' or disengaged which can then lead to problematic behaviour seeping in. This is not to say that there shouldn't be changes and new starting points within the lesson. Fresh starts within the lesson are crucial. We all know that continuing with any one task for too long can lead to inattention and boredom. It is the same for pupils, and when pupils are bored that's when things become behaviourally problematic. Having several 'starts' and new learning episodes in lessons is critical to good learning, creating a strong routine and leading to good behaviour.

The **ends of lessons** can also be a behaviour flashpoint, or reflection. Ending lessons in an orderly, well-structured way, celebrating what has been learnt and leaving the individuals in the class in a positive frame of mind to continue with the rest of their learning day is so important. If the lesson concludes in a calm, positive way, then we as teachers also feel ready for the rest of the day and the challenges it might bring.

Successful teachers also know that setting homework, for example, is not always best served right at the end of the lesson. This is because it can often be rushed and can lead to misunderstanding and confusion – leading to incomplete or 'forgotten' homework and future behaviour flashpoints. Taking time to set homework during an earlier part of the lesson, perhaps midway, allows for any clarifications from pupils to be answered and makes it much more likely that it will be understood and completed (thereby avoiding other behaviour issues).

The goal is to manage procedures like setting homework, tidying up and pulling the lesson together in a way that is both efficient and effective. I have observed many primary teachers, and some secondary school teachers, using music with a cheerful upbeat tempo to help pupils have a focused approach to tidying up. Particularly when they have engaged in a practical task and there is a lot of 'resetting' needed in the classroom. Popular choices include 'William Tell Overture' by Rossini and 'Flight of the Bumblebee' by Rimsky-Korsakov. Pupils enjoy finishing up what they are working on, tidying and returning resources and it helps create some urgency in pupil behaviour, without the need to strain your voice. One teacher told me: like Pavlov's dog, as soon as her class hear the first bars of music from a specific song, they automatically start busying themselves sorting out their materials. Using music purposefully as a tool to influence behaviour really helps. Creating these habits creates a positive routine around tidying up. Developing different ways of influencing pupils' behaviour like this is really helpful to get the desired effect without any stress.

> **Research nugget**
>
> 'Researchers estimate that 40 to 50 per cent of our actions on any given day are done out of habit...' (Clear, 2018, P. 160). If, as teachers we can get our pupils into the right learning and behaviour habits then lessons will run more smoothly. Likewise, if pupils are not taught to develop these pathways, including getting ready for their lesson quickly and quietly or raising their hand when asking a question, then conflict can arise.

In lessons that run like clockwork, there are usually well understood procedures for dealing with the 'bumps' in the road. The goal is to have well established, smooth procedures for dealing with minor disruptions like pupils not having the correct pen or resource so that the lesson does not get derailed by these elements. Great teachers think ahead and envisage these predictable scenarios and implement strategies for dealing with them with minimum fuss. These might involve keeping a spare set of resources in a specific place, or other strategies such as pupils being expected to borrow from a friend first.

Now we've considered the role of rules and routines in the smooth running of lessons, and we've thought about our goals for this area. It is also important to think about what happens when things go askew. What role do sanctions play here?

Rule breakers and sanctions

Rules, of course, go hand in hand with sanctions – although the real goal of setting rules is to make them clear, understandable and transparent, to encourage pupils not to break them in the first place and avoiding incurring any sanctions at all! Once we get to the point that we are giving out lots of sanctions then really they are not doing what we hoped them to do, and the sanctions are no deterrent. However, if pupils know that if they choose to break a rule, for example, not completing classwork or exhibiting poor behaviour, that their teacher will fairly enforce the sanction, and not forget or be disorganised, then they soon learn that it is far better to play by the rules, rather than hope to break them and avoid consequences.

We must have planned sanctions, of course, as all actions have consequences, but the goal should be that they should not need enforcing frequently – like the traffic fines and point systems that threaten to deal with the careless or dangerous driver. We want the pupils to abide by the rules, but to ensure they are very clear about what will happen if they don't follow them.

Many schools have 'steps', 'stages' or numbered consequences when dealing with low-level disruptive behaviour; a bit like points on a driving licence! This is the sort of behaviour, which is often frustrating to teachers and other learners, but not dangerous or highly serious. Low-level disruptive behaviour might include: persistent talking, calling out, not getting on with the classwork, etc. Pupils are often told that they have a Level 1 reprimand and there are clear well-defined steps which if the behaviour is not amended then a more serious consequence will follow. For minor infractions these might include moving seats or a loss of certain privileges. More serious sanctions might include a detention, conversation with parents/carers or going on a report card. Initially Level 1 behaviour issues are usually dealt with by the class teacher and this helps establish them as the person in charge of the behaviour in their class.

Ideally, we want to try other tactics first to prevent the difficult behaviour occurring in the first place. But it is important that when we get to the stage of issuing a consequence – to give the 'consequence' in a way that suggests regret – rather than the *'Ha I gotcha!'* gleeful approach that I have seen in some instances. It is much better to give the impression that you are giving the punishment (which is after all what a consequence is) with sad regret that the pupil has *chosen* to take this path, rather than looking like a spiteful teacher who is pleased to have 'caught out' the pupil in their wrongdoing. This later creates an adversarial approach where the pupil will see you as the enemy, or someone who derives pleasure from enforcing the rules. Grudges can really fester and do nothing for classroom relationships. These teaching behaviours also suggest a lack of control of emotions which is never a good thing in lessons. We need to make sure that we appear calm and measured as this is a key way of de-escalating the high emotions that the pupils might be experiencing. If their emotions are very high, then giving them any strong reaction in return can really make things much worse. A teacher sounding gleeful or doling out punishments in anger is like throwing petrol on a fire that is already smouldering! If a pupil persistently fails to respond to the first level of sanctions set by the teacher, for example, persistently calling out, then the pupil might be set a detention and the middle leader or pastoral staff will often be involved to help support this.

There are some behaviours which are so poor or dangerous that they should obviously bypass the first staging approach. These include things such as being defiant, refusing to follow critical instructions, swearing at staff, refusing to complete work, behaviours that put themselves and/or others in danger and persistent behaviour that does not respond to the staged consequences. The response should be escalated to follow the school's published behaviour system. This is often removal from class through an on-call system by a senior member of staff and/or subsequent further punishments or contact with parents/carers. Often the Head of Year or Head of House will be involved, as frequently, such poor behaviour might be widespread or have other implications.

If a pupil has to be removed from class, you as the teacher should action this very calmly. The rest of the class will be watching you closely, by remaining in control – even when your heart is pounding – is the very best thing to do. You should not be afraid to take this step if it is required. Some pupils can sense that a teacher is reluctant to let other senior staff know that there are behaviour issues in class and try and cover things up for too long. This can really undermine you in the eyes of the pupils – don't be afraid to use the school's behaviour policy, after, of course, ensuring that you have done the best you can at the lower stages first. Sometimes, despite your best-efforts things will need external assistance and acknowledging this is the first step to improving behaviour. Whatever behaviour we accept in the lesson without dealing with sets the standard for behaviour from then on, so we must think carefully about our actions in response to difficult behaviour.

The ultimate goal is that with effective behaviour management the need to escalate situations is much reduced. When you act calmly, clearly and consistently you can prevent difficult behaviour from getting to this stage. We will explore strategies for helping you manage this in the rest of the chapter. But let's first look at the reality of the situation regarding rules and routines. Are you ready to reflect?

Reality: your current situation regarding rules and routines

Which of the pictures below would your pupils pick to represent your approach to rules and routines?

Figure 3: Open road with some signage   Figure 4: Lego pieces

Figure 5: Rainforest bridge   Figure 6: Hawk on a branch

Why have you selected this picture?
What do you think it reveals about your behaviour management style?
Are you happy with this? Which picture would you **most like** to represent your reality?
What is working well?
What could be better?

Key questions to ask yourself

1 Are you clear on your rules in your lesson? Are your pupils clear too? Have you asked them? Do they understand the reasons behind the rules?

2 Do you follow through on your rules – even if it is inconvenient to yourself? For example, talking to a pupil at break time or contacting a parent to discuss the issues?

3 Do you give any sanctions with obvious regret? Are they appropriate and do you find that increasingly you are giving out far fewer sanctions – especially to the same pupils because the situation is improving and they know that you will enforce reasonable standards of behaviour?

4 If pupils are in detention, do you take the opportunities to have conversations to try and rebuild the relationship and help foster better habits?

5 Do pupils believe that you act fairly and with consideration? Do parents/carers?

6 Do you have clear and effective systems and routines in class? Are you consistent with these?

7 Are your class clear about the routines you have?

8 Do changes and transitions in your lessons work smoothly?

9 Do you review, tweak and change your routines/rules if you feel that they could be improved?

10 Are you following the guidance and ethos of your school/college in the way you use rules, rewards and routines?

11 Do you have clear starts and ends of lessons? Are these managed calmly and positively?

12 Do you have effective strategies for setting and collecting homework?

13 Do you have effective communication with pastoral staff/heads of key stage/department if you are having persistent difficulties with a specific pupil's behaviour?

14 Do you contact parents/carers before problems become deeply embedded?

Opportunities: making improvements with rules and routines

As a teacher you are not an island, your school will have some over-arching guidance and rules compiled within a School Behaviour Policy. There will often be common routines that you are expected to abide by, support and instil into your class as part of school-wide policy. These might need to be contextualised by the year group or subject you are teaching. You would expect all classes within the same primary school to uphold the fundamental values which govern the school, such as mutual respect and responsibility even if the specific details of these rules might be very different between Year 6 and Reception, because of the different ages of the pupils.

On occasion, you might not agree with the school rules, and for this reason it is especially important to try to get a good feel for them during school interviews, and via the school website, policies and inspection reports. Consistency (within context) is an important way that schools can ensure good behaviour across the school, and so it is important to work in one whose systems you can support and enforce. It can feel very uncomfortable if you find that you are in a school having to enforce rules that you feel are particularly Draconian or nonsensical.

Real life cameo

I worked for a year in an acting Middle Leadership role in a school that had some very deeply entrenched whole school behavioural issues. These were not always acknowledged or resolved by the school's leadership. I vividly remember, as a new member of staff, helping a colleague manage the behaviour of a boy who had been very disruptive in her class. He had been incredibly challenging across the school, and he was firmly on the SLT's radar. However, I remember being completely dismayed that when the Headteacher ambled past – instead of offering support to a very demanding situation, he firmly rebuked both me and my colleague in front of the student! The reason? The young man we were dealing with wasn't following 'short-sleeve orders' that had supposedly been decreed earlier that week! These 'critical' uniform rules (which seemed to focus solely on whether blazers and ties should be worn in summertime) had never been communicated to either of us new staff before we started! And of course, the Headteacher was avoiding dealing with the more pressing and difficult issue with the student who was outside of his lesson owing to severely disruptive behaviour!

Clear uniform rules, and their reinforcement, can of course be helpful and support an orderly learning environment. Although I am often impressed on my trips to the United States to see the quality of learning and behaviour that can be achieved when there are zero uniform regulations and students happily learn wearing sports clothes, oversized hoodies and jeans. Clarity regarding uniform rules can transmit one sign of high standards. However, sometimes an unrelenting focus on minor uniform infractions are common because it is much easier for senior leaders to deal with a slightly wrong style of haircut, or shoes with a hint of a logo rather than the more pressing and challenging issues of improving teaching, learning and pupils' attitudes. These would ultimately have improved behaviour more thoroughly in the long term.

So, we need to make sure that we are supporting the school-wide behaviour policy – even if we have not created it ourselves and may not always agree with every aspect. It is important to focus on the areas that we do have control over. This brings me to one of the key opportunities in managing behaviour via your own classroom rules. Below are some suggestions for how to maximise your expertise in the area of rules and routines:

- **Clarity: ensure that rules are communicated to pupils with crystal clear clarity.**

    Even as adults, we dislike getting called out for breaking rules. We feel even more aggrieved if we did not know about the rules, understand them or if the details related to them were unclear. You've read about the grudge I held regarding the 'shirt sleeve orders rule' and that was over a decade ago! Figure 7 shows a clear set of rules and expectations displayed in a ladies' toilet in a pub in a 'lively' part of my local town. There is absolute clarity about what rule breakers should expect, that if someone was caught doing any of the mentioned activities they could hardly be surprised by the consequences. The language and the outcomes are unequivocal. Whilst I'm not advocating similar signs, it is important that pupils are clear about what the both the rules are and any consequences for breaking them.

- **Transparency: pupils should be clearly informed about what is expected of them**.

    Travelling through Clapham Junction train station, I'm always struck by how helpfully the direction rules are displayed. The visual display using arrows and green/red colour coding is much more effective than just a sign telling people where to walk. And importantly it works! Of course, I'm not suggesting you go around colour coding things, (although a friend has colour coded trays in her classroom so that pupils can drop off their homework in the correct one – she swears by it!) But making the rules transparent and being super clear about exactly what you are expecting helps everybody do what you want them to because it's so obvious. There's no excuse for not complying.

- **Meaning: explain rules and their rationale clearly to pupils so that they understand.**

    It is written in the job of the teenager that they should sneer and scorn at rules. Even younger pupils who are sometimes (mistakenly) believed to be more easily influenced by adults ask the question: 'why?' repeatedly when we ask them to do something. We will have much greater adherence to the rules if pupils can understand **why exactly** they are being asked to follow them. Often, as the experienced adult it is so obvious why pupils in the science lab should have long hair tied back, and wear safety goggles and that bags be placed under chairs, that we forget to communicate this 'why' to pupils. We take it for granted that it will be as obvious to them as it is to us. I observed a heated discussion between some GCSE pupils about the fact that they weren't allowed in the gym without adult supervision and how unfair it was because they wanted to go at a specific time after school. They didn't understand the why (health and safety issues related to heavy equipment). If students can appreciate and understand the 'why' behind rules, then they are often more ready to accept them.

Figure 7: Drug-taking policy sign (C. Bentley-Davies as photographer)

Figure 8: Station staircase directions (C. Bentley-Davies as photographer)

Should you construct rules of the classroom together with your class?

Some teachers swear by this – but it is not something that I usually do. This mainly involves discussing and agreeing the rules *with* the pupils. I prefer not to do this because the class is not a democracy – the teacher is in charge. I prefer to think of it as a benign dictatorship. The teacher needs to be the one to set the rules – however it is important that the rules make sense and seem reasonable to the pupils and one of the ways of doing this is to ensure that the rationale for each rule is clear and obvious.

What if there is no 'why'?

When you set a rule, think about what you are trying to achieve. Petty rules are never good rules – neither are they easy to uphold. However sometimes we must enforce a rule that the school has that you aren't personally fussed about. For example, students having to take off their coats in the depths of winter when the heating feels like it is barely working. In this case it can feel hard to defend this rule. I tackle this with a three-part approach, saying:

> *'I appreciate that you feel cold…'* **(1. Acknowledging their viewpoint)**
> *'But the school rule is: no coats indoors…'* **(2. Reassertion of the rule)**
> *'So I'd appreciate you taking your coat off now.'* **(3. Follow up with clear direction)**

Notice that you are deferring to the 'school' rule rather than saying it's your rule and avoiding getting into a heated debate with the student about how sensible that rule is. Then give a brief (intentional) **pause**. Often this is enough to resolve the issue and the pause gives the student sufficient time to take their coat off (and save face with their peers). It also literally gives a breathing space for both participants to help de-escalate the situation. If they are a little reluctant, the follow up, *'I'd appreciate you taking your coat off **now**'* offers a clear, polite direction, which should be said very crisply – you aren't opening a debate. You are issuing an instruction. I found that having some 'scripts' to approach tricky situations is very helpful. You can use these in a multitude of contexts relating to rules and it might help to practise them beforehand so that you sound calm and in control.

Pause for thought

- What are the behaviour flashpoints in your class? Could they be helped by the three-part script approach mentioned above?
- Do you have any useful stock phrases or scripts that you use?

I think the success in this approach largely stems from the opening acknowledgement of the other person's point of view. Even though you are going to ask them to do something that they don't want to do, it will result in a more positive reaction. Acknowledging their point of view disarms them and makes them feel that their 'issue' has been seen by you. It also gives them the sense that they have not lost face with their peers when they actually do what you have asked them to. The concern about their friends' reaction is sadly much often more important to them than their relationship with you, particularly at secondary school or college.

'I appreciate…but the rule is… thank you'

To summarise:

- Avoid unnecessary rules and those that are unduly complex. Keep it clear and simple. Avoid hastily coming up with completely foolish rules (often uttered in frustration) such as 'the next person who speaks will be in detention!' You can absolutely guarantee it will be a lovely student who is simply asking a friend if they can borrow their ruler rather than a pupil who has been testing your limits all morning. And then you are in a very awkward position!
- Load the dice in your favour. Don't expect pupils to work in silence for too long. Having unrealistic expectations leads to disaster. Pupils (and in fact adults of all ages) will struggle to maintain focus and work silently for too long. Build in pockets of time when pupils know that they will get the opportunity to have some structured discussion, then you will find there is less likelihood of them becoming disruptive.

'Now everyone. I'd like you to work very quietly on solving those problems. In just 15 minutes, we will discuss the ones you are finding tricky. Remember, if you get stuck don't worry. Just start tackling the next one and make a note of the ones that are problematic. Off you go.'

Here the pupils know that they will not be expected to work in silence for a sustained period of time and the teacher has showed empathy and given direction about what to do if they find the work difficult.

> ### Real life cameo
>
> Like most of us, I'm not somebody who wants a lot of drama or conflict in my day-to-day life. When I've done something wrong, I'm pretty reasonable in admitting to and taking the consequences. But I've had many encounters with train companies in recent years, and I've often been threatened with fines and admonished for having the wrong ticket. Usually I take it on the chin, but I tend to check and seek advice from train staff before boarding and paying for tickets – and still sometimes get told I've bought the wrong ticket! Just when I thought I had a handle on the rules I find out something new, for example, that on Fridays the rules are different – but not all Fridays! The complexity, and often puzzling nature of the rail rules, not to mention the rules sometimes only being visible in very small print online, can cause my usually sanguine attitude to become riled. On one occasion I refused to buy another ticket – and luckily because it was a Friday I didn't have to! My point being: keep things simple and have great clarity in your rules!

Opportunities: Sanctions and resetting expectations

Nobody (ourselves included) wants to spend time in detention. Who wants to miss a bit of break or lunchtime? However, if you are setting your own sanctions or pupils are in a detention with you, then this can be a golden opportunity to reset expectations and build a better relationship. Doing so without a huge audience (which can sometimes fan poor behaviour) makes this much more likely to be successful.

This is one of the main reasons why I have always been in favour of holding my own detentions, rather than placing pupils into a centralised school detention. Of course, as a Middle Leader, I was also a person who oversaw detentions for the team. When the staff member who had set the detention took the time to talk to the pupil first (even if they did not supervise the whole detention) without fail this often led to improved subsequent behaviour. It showed that the staff member was invested and would make an effort. I noticed fewer frequent fliers in detentions with those staff members. Investing the time really does pay dividends.

Explore, discuss, refocus and repair

When I *have* had pupils in detention for problematic behaviour, the opportunity to explore the reasons behind their behaviour and to plan a way forward has led not only to improved behaviours in lessons, but a reparation of the pupil/teacher relationship. I have always tried to discuss their behaviour reasonably with them, to explore why they might have been 'acting out' or why they have failed to complete yet another piece of homework. I also impressed upon them that the reason that I was bothering with them was because I could see that they had real potential – which they weren't yet reaching. Most children will give a grudging respect to a teacher who *always* follows through.

Real life cameo

Over dinner, one of my friends mentioned that a boy in her GCSE class was capable but seemed 'allergic' to completing homework. He complained once: *'but Miss you are the only teacher who bothers. I haven't done my Maths or French homework for months. I don't get homework detentions from them.'* Over time (and it took many months apparently) he started completing the homework she had set because he said it was less bother than if he didn't; he knew she would always follow through. Sadly, when the GCSE results came out the only two subjects that he achieved his potential in was those she taught.

Holding pupils, to account for their behaviour takes time and effort – but it really reaps rewards. Putting in a lot of time at the start means that you can ease off once the behaviour improves. You can then also give out praise, rewards and notice the improved efforts which will further build the improved behaviour.

It is worth thinking about what sort of activities pupils will undertake in detention. If they are in detention for a lack of work completed in lessons or as homework, then it is fair enough to get them to complete work in detention. Sometimes you might discover that they have found the work particularly tricky and therefore there is a good opportunity to 'reteach' or support them with this. It is never a good idea to set extra curriculum work for poor behaviour detentions because this associates academic work with punishment and can further deepen their hostility to your lessons.

Sometimes, during conversations with pupils in detention I have discovered reasons behind their behaviour that I was completely unaware of and we have found ways to work with that pupil to help improve their behaviour. These have included:

- A Year 8 pupil who had not been completing homework and who was forgetting equipment as a result of having to spend time between her divorcing parents' two addresses. She was under considerable stress managing this and being used as 'go between' behind two hostile parents. We managed to get her a single locker in both the lower school and upper school so that she could leave some equipment at school to help her manage some of these issues.
- A new student who had anxiety about joining in during lessons and reading aloud who chose to be disruptive rather than to be put on the spot. In this situation the student was allowed to acclimatise to the class before being asked to read aloud. She was also given very short extracts to read until her confidence increased. She was also praised when she did participate and this encouraged her to want to join in more.
- A boy who was never provided with breakfast at home, so came into school finding it difficult to focus. He was able to join a breakfast club to ensure that he had something to eat in the morning. Additionally, his teacher checked in with him early in the day to ensure that he had eaten.

Sometimes, of course, there might be serious safeguarding issues and your job is not to probe or investigate these but to pass them on immediately to the school's designated safeguarding officer/leader.

Research nugget

The power of fitting in should not be underestimated and we need to use this to our advantage in lessons. Pupils, like all of us, look to how others are behaving as a guidance on how *they* should behave. Psychologist Solomon Asch conducted a serious of experiments in 1951 to investigate how group pressure influences an individual's judgement. In trials, participants were given a task where the correct answer was obvious. However, when they were placed with 'pretend actor' participants who deliberately gave an incorrect answer, many participants followed suit. By the end of the experiment, 75 per cent of participants had agreed with the group answer even though it was obviously incorrect (Asch, 1951).

Humans are animals and 'the normal behaviour of the tribe often overpowers the desired behaviour of the individual' (Clear, 2018, P.120). For example, one study found that when a chimpanzee learns an effective way to crack nuts open as a member of one group and then switches to become part of a new group that uses a less effective strategy, the chimpanzee will avoid using the superior nut cracking method just to blend in with the rest of the chimps. Humans are similar (Clear, 2018, P.120).

Real life cameo

A pupil told me that he felt immense peer pressure to mess around and be 'a lad' with his friends when in lessons. He was a very popular boy, and he once asked: *'Miss, can you actually move me to sit on my own? I can do my work that way and concentrate. I do really want to do well, but…'* When I told him that yes, he could just sit at the front next lesson, he told me I was missing the point. *'It's got to come from you Miss, and I must be publicly told off and moved!'* Peer pressure matters.

Pupils will follow the lead of others which is why it is far more effective to look for pupils who are in fact following the rules and mention this. For example: *'Well done – I can see that Jakob, Frankie, and Usam have made a good start …'* This increases the peer pressure to improve in a positive way. It tells the class that others have started and gives those that haven't a firm direction that they need to start working now. It is a lighter and more productive way of achieving compliance to rules, rather than always looking for those who do not conform and by pointing this out to the class. Being called out in public can lead to pupils feeling embarrassed and sometimes angry. It also tells the class that not following the rules is a viable option because others are not yet co-operating. This is clearly not what you want. It can feel hard to focus on the positives – but it really does work!

If pupils are creating low level behaviour issues it is often useful to give them the opportunity to adjust their behaviour first. For example, through using your body language to highlight that you have spotted them not following the rules (we will cover body language in the next chapter). Reactions such as a raised eyebrow or brief eye contact can be useful in showing pupils that you've clocked them misbehaving without drawing everyone's attention to it. The next step is getting a little bit physically closer to them (not too much!) just walking in their general direction, perhaps, or having a brief word – but then give them a moment to amend their behaviour rather than directly issuing sanctions.

If you are teaching at secondary level and you find some pupils or a class tricky then it can be incredibly useful to observe these pupils in another lesson, with another teacher. It is likely that if they are behaving well there will be some techniques or strategies that the teacher is using that you can employ. Talking to the teacher or the teaching assistant can provide useful insight. Sometimes we can get locked into patterns of behaviour with a pupil. Seeing them acting differently in another class, watching the teacher de-escalate or have a different relationship with them or perhaps getting them to work with other pupils can be game changers. Make sure that you are also as clued up as you can be about any SEND or physical needs and be aware of any pastoral concerns or changes in home life that could be causing an impact on behaviour.

Way forward

Having read this chapter you will have received some suggestions about rules and routines. It is worth looking at your current rules and routines with fresh eyes. Remember, if you are teaching secondary or college aged students, that they might be facing a wide range of routines and rules that they are expected to follow. In secondary school they might have up to ten separate teachers – all with slightly different directives. If you are looking to change things, think very clearly about the process and remember new routines and systems take a while to work – it is in this transition phase that you really need to be persistent. In a primary school context think about the different rules you set across the different subjects you teach and whether specific behaviour challenges arise in each subject.

Areas that I think are working well with my classes/ individuals are:

_____
_____
_____
_____
_____
_____
_____

Areas I would like to work on relating to rules and routines:

1 _____

2 _____

3 _____

The planned actions I am going to take are:

1 _____

2 _____

3 _____

Review: How did it go? What did I learn? What are my reflections? Am I going to keep any new strategies? Do I have any further steps? Do I need to seek support/advice from elsewhere?

4 I see you: the importance of non-verbal communication

How important do you think **body language** is in managing behaviour? Where would you rate it on a scale from zero (completely unimportant) to ten (critically important)? If you've given it less than a seven then you're in good company. Many teachers I train don't initially think it is *that* vital. But here's the thing – it really is! Getting body language right, (or non-verbal communication as it is sometimes known), is one of my top three critical strategies in the behaviour toolkit. If we can present ourselves in a way that inspires confidence and understands the non-verbal behaviour of others, we have an invaluable skill – without even having to open our mouths!

I didn't realise how important body language was until I started mentoring teachers in my own school. I gradually realised the effect that it had on pupils but this wasn't properly crystallised for me until I had the pleasure of travelling around the UK and overseas demonstrating teaching, running revision lessons and visiting different settings. It was only then I truly came to understand that some micro behaviours I was exhibiting, when meeting new classes, were either really hindering me or helping me. Once I knew this, I could fine tune them to ensure that individuals were behaving well – so then I could teach them the great revision lessons I had planned and they would *engage in the learning* rather than looking for an opportunity to disrupt the task.

Likewise, observing new teachers, I saw that although they might have a great lesson plan, if their behaviour and body language did not instil confidence then the class would be *much* harder to manage. The pupils would pick up on their nervousness and lack of confidence and the behaviour of the class would start to deteriorate.

Real life cameo

An Early Career Teacher recently told me that when teaching his new Year 7 class, he overheard one of them talking and realised that he needed to make a few tiny changes to instil confidence.

> *'I had my lesson plan on a sheet of A4 and I was holding it as I was teaching. As I was holding it, it moved about a lot because my hand was almost imperceptibly shaking. One of the Year 7's at the front said to his neighbour: "It's because he's a new teacher – he's nervous..." This was a sweet Year 7 class that weren't going to cause me any behaviour problems,'* he continued, *'but I realised that I did the very same thing with my rowdy GCSE class – and of course I looked nervous and ill at ease. No wonder they felt they could mess about without any issues. Now I make sure that my plan is either on the side edge of my desk within easy sight or attached to a firm clip board that doesn't flap about when I hold it, and it makes me appear more confident.'* These are simple changes but make a significant difference in how you appear to your class.

Goal: communicating non-verbally through body language

Research nugget

Researcher Albert Mehrabian reported that 55 per cent of a message's impact is communicated by facial cues, while 38 per cent is communicated by the voice tone and other vocal characteristics. Only seven per cent is actually communicated by the actual words used (Mehrabian, 1971).

Let's think about our goal for exhibiting great non-verbal communication and let's unpick what is looks like day-to-day in school or college. Body language or non-verbal communication are all the signs and responses we make when we are in the presence of others. These include how we stand, how we move, how we hold ourselves; our gestures, our facial expressions, and how we adjust our clothing and accessories. There's quite a list. Many of these things we do completely unconsciously, for example, giving a tiny frown when we read something we disagree with or when take a bite out of something that isn't to our taste.

Although we might not always be aware of these responses, when we are teaching there are 30 pairs of eyes watching us and responding to our non-verbal signals. Whilst pupils are unlikely to accurately articulate *exactly* what it is about your body language that make you seem confident or otherwise, they will definitely notice. And most importantly this will influence whether they will behave *or not*!

Similarly, a teacher skilled in non-verbal communication knowledge is also observing, evaluating, and reviewing the non-verbal behaviour of their pupils as they teach so that they can intervene *before* Chloe passes a note, or Diynah stops working or Ethan tries to draw on his neighbour's work. A skilled behaviourist is clued up to read the signs in the room to know when *exactly* to stop the lesson for a mini-review because they can see some puzzled expressions. Or when to smile encouragingly at a pupil who looks anxious, or when to raise an eyebrow at a pupil who is just reaching in their bag to… Noticing the non-verbal behaviour signals of others allows us to pre-empt and redirect the tricky behaviour before it starts. Great body language is about both being inwardly aware of our own body language and how we are feeling, *and* outwardly conscious of what it is communicating to others. It sounds complex – but trust me, there are a few key things that can make the world of difference in how you are perceived by your class and how reading the body language of others can help you manage your lessons much more smoothly.

Think for a moment about a teacher you've seen around school who has great presence. You might not have even spoken to them but they exude confidence, control and poise. You feel certain that their classes are well controlled and enjoyable for both pupils and the staff member. Note that these aren't always people with acknowledged outwardly high status like the Headteacher or Assistant Headteacher – they can be quite a junior member of staff with great non-verbal communication. What is it about the person you have thought of that makes you believe: *'I bet they are in control'* and *'I bet their lessons are enjoyable and well-received'*? How do they hold themselves and move about the school, as they interact with others?

Mastering your non-verbal communication skills

I often arrive at schools very early (because I am concerned about finding them easily!) so I have plenty of time to observe other teachers' non-verbal communication before the day even starts. I watch some teachers stroll into school, looking around them, happy to be there. They greet and nod to pupils as they make their way into the buildings, making brief eye contact. I've seen the same teachers walk purposefully around the school – owning the space – and they look filled with confidence and assurance. They pick up firmly but positively on any behaviour infractions that they see. It comes as little surprise to me when I observe their lessons to see that they are well ordered and have a warm classroom climate. The behaviour we see in our lessons is influenced by how we act and react around the school. Pupils observe how we behave and respond accordingly.

These teachers manage transitions between different parts of the lesson effectively. They seem to have a knack of nipping difficult behaviour in the bud before it really starts – often by using a subtle gesture. Endings of lessons are also calm, and the teacher ensures that the class leaves in a positive frame of mind.

It's important, however, to add some comments about non-verbal communication that is beyond our own personal control. For example, I make mention of many ways we can move and control our non-verbal communication to influence others. But of course, there are disabilities, physical injuries and other reasons that might mean following this advice is not always possible. We must always bear this in mind and adapt accordingly. For example, a student who does not make eye contact when answering a question might not be being deliberately rude. Maybe they are excruciatingly shy or neurodivergent. We need to be alert to these possibilities and have an awareness that not everyone uses the same non-verbal cues, and therefore be careful about what we insist on. For this reason, I will not insist that everybody always gives full eye contact, as I know that this can be very alarming for some pupils. I will however want to see that they are paying attention to the lesson and are engaging in the learning, but I will use other ways of checking on this (such as questioning) rather than just relying on eye contact alone. So even though being aware of our posture and facial expressions is important, it's not the only way we can obtain our goal of great non-verbal communication. Being aware of outside factors such as the way we're made up as a person, different cultures and personal experiences are crucial in understanding how to achieve the best non-verbal communication we can.

Real life cameo

> I remember offering to shake hands with a male teacher who I was working with. I had not met him before and was doing this in an attempt to show a positive, friendly manner – however it was rebuffed! I later found out that this was because of his religious observances.

I was completely unaware of this at the time. I felt quite embarrassed that I did not know this and apologised. There are a variety of ways to set a friendly atmosphere without handshaking, and this was a lesson I learnt that day that I am now mindful of. Some cultures, religions and individuals will have certain gestures and body language customs that will influence how they behave and how they interpret our interactions. I always do my best to research them, especially when working overseas, but sometimes mistakes are made with our communication despite our best intentions!

Real life cameo

A couple of years ago I had major abdominal surgery and my ability to walk confidently and move easily was severely compromised for several months. My posture was hunched, and my facial expressions often revealed my extreme discomfort. I had a fair bit of time off work and could have taken much longer. But I was chomping at the bit to get back to visiting colleges. I felt emotionally ready and felt I could manage some days, but I felt that I would be unable to stand for any extended length of time. I had always seen the importance of being able to walk around the room freely checking on pupils, and physically owning the space by standing tall, so how would I manage? I spoke to a sixth form college that I visit regularly. We had several big events planned. I explained that I felt ready to do the events but would have real trouble standing for more than ten minutes at a time. We agreed that I could sit on a stool in the middle of the front of the room, and with trepidation off I went. Everything went incredibly well. Afterwards speaking to the organiser, I expressed surprise that without moving I still felt I could manage the room effectively and control proceedings. She reacted with surprise at my doubts, explaining that my gestures with my hands, and use of eye contact had been so effective. It seemed that these non-verbal signals had effectively replaced the role of walking around the room. Not everyone will use the same non-verbal gestures but we can all still 'own' our space and command with our presence.

Reality: your body language

Look at the 'body language quadrant' and read through the different zones. Take a moment to reflect on your previous years of teaching and how the different zones may apply to you. If you're new to teaching, you could apply this to everyday life.

The body language quadrant

Zone A	Zone B
Confident high-status and positive non-verbal communication	**Arrogant high-status and aggressive non-verbal communication**
• Good posture, standing tall and owning the space. • Greeting with brief, positive eye contact – smile and poised body language – using expansive body language to include the whole class. E.g. sweeping eyes across the room. • Awareness of own facial expressions, smiling, as appropriate. If frowning it is done deliberately (and very briefly) as a way of telling a pupil that off-task behaviour has been noted. Then positive body language resumed. • Open use of hand gestures as appropriate. • Overall impression: a confident, assertive, happy teacher who is in charge.	• Clear posture but blocking or standing in the way of others, or standing far too close to them. • Refusing eye contact, looking far above the pupils or holding eye contact for too long which creates a hostile and aggressive atmosphere. • Facial expressions do not attempt to hide negative emotions, e.g. frowns, sneers, etc. Tension can be seen around the mouth and jaw. • Hand gestures can be sharp and combative. These can be quite sudden or they show tension such as holding hand in a tight fist or moving the hand in a slicing/chopping motion. • Overall impression: a superior and/or potentially unpredictable and quick to anger. The teacher might appear as lacking in confidence by overusing aggressive body language which can dangerously inflame already tense situations.

Zone C	Zone D
Low-status/submissive and non-verbal communication that doesn't quite succeed in being positive	**Low-status and negative non-verbal communication**
<ul><li>Sitting or standing sideways on, or at the periphery of the room, rather than facing directly. Trying to stay on the side lines to avoid taking up too much room. This shows a lack of confidence.</li><li>Not making eye contact – or eyes very lowered.</li><li>Giving nervous quick smiles that seem insincere.</li><li>Using objects as a barrier, such as a desk.</li><li>Self-grooming, touching hair/neck/possessions in a way that suggests that they are ill-at-ease.</li><li>Overall impression: a teacher who is trying to create a positive atmosphere but lacks confidence.</li></ul>	<ul><li>Slouching and holding something across the body like folded arms or a book to act as a defence barrier or for comfort.</li><li>Not making confident eye contact. Sometimes showing dismissive body language such as rolling eyes at pupils' comments or narrowing them when something has been said that they don't agree with.</li><li>Unsmiling.</li><li>Obvious clock watching.</li><li>Overall impression: a teacher who doesn't want to be in the lesson and who doesn't enjoy teaching (this class) or maybe any at all!</li></ul>

Zone A – the ideal!

We want to show that we are assertive and in control but that we are also welcoming and inclusive to everyone in our lesson. The vibe we want to give off is that we are positive and happy to be there, and that we are confident and in control of what we are doing. We **expect** compliance and that pupils will engage with and enjoy the lesson as much as we are, and our non-verbal cues should reinforce this.

Zone B

One example of non-verbal communication we wish to avoid. This is a highly inflammatory situation where the body language verges on aggressive as we try to rule with fear. To rule with fear can make difficult situations so much worse.

Zone C

If we're showing passivity and timidity, pupils won't think twice about misbehaving. Although there are some *almost* positive non-verbal behaviours in Zone C, they are not 'owned' by us, the teacher. Therefore, the pupils do not feel entirely convinced by you, for example, nervous smiling. The Zone C quadrant is too apologetic – the behaviours are saying 'please behave and like me.' We are not owning the lesson and therefore appear passive.

Zone D

We've become passive aggressive, and we also come from a place of negativity and hostility! I'm sure we can all remember being at school and feeling that a teacher didn't like being there and didn't know how to control us – well this is evident in this quadrant. Non-verbal signs such as eye-rolling, sighing, shrugging and other frustrated and despairing gestures don't inspire confidence and are best avoided. If you've ever had a friend or colleague give an eye roll or sign when you are talking or when you're in their presence, you will know how corrosive these non-verbal signals can be!

Slight variations of behaviours can make or break the pupils' view of the teacher. We need to aim for being 'confident with high-status' and using 'positive non-verbal communication' found in Zone A.

Interesting nugget

World famous singer and musician Elvis Presley captivated huge audiences across the world. He was an accomplished performer and really owned his body language, exuding confidence and enjoyment in his work. On a visit to Graceland, my tour guide revealed that when Elvis first started performing his leg would wobble uncontrollably through the stress of being on stage in front of big groups of people. This made him look ill at ease and like a nervous young horse struggling to stand. He was advised to 'own' this body language if he could not remove it and make it more positive. His wobbling leg became an exaggerated, confident move and part of his iconic performance and swagger.

This is a reminder that we don't have to feel confident – but we do have to act as if we are confident. It's a reminder to own our body language and be aware of how things are perceived. When you take your jacket off because you are uncomfortably hot, you could squirm out of it and look ruffled or you could calmly and confidently remove it. I observed a science teacher start talking to his class explaining the objectives of what they would be doing that lesson. As he spoke – he calmly removed his jacket and slowly rolled up his shirt sleeves, arm by arm. It was measured, controlled and he spoke whilst doing so. He was non-verbally telling the class – *'it's time to start working – I'm working hard too… Let's roll up our sleeves… and crack on'*. It was calm, controlled and purposeful! The same actions done in slightly different ways give completely different impressions, turning a weakness into a strength.

Now that you're familiar with the different types of body language and their positive or negative connotations, take this moment to further reflect on the questions below.

1 Which behaviour body language quadrant do you think you operate in most of the time? Does it differ depending on the class/subject or time of day?
2 How do you greet your class at the start of the lesson?
3 When you are giving instructions how do you create an impression of positive knowledgeable authority?
4 Are you aware of how your body language changes when you feel under pressure?
5 Are you aware of any habits or giveaway signs you have? (such as covering your mouth if you are not really meaning what you are saying or shaking your head minimally whilst saying: *'I'm really enjoying this meal'*.)
6 What are you are your body language strengths?
7 Do you think that you have any areas to work on?
8 Have you asked any of your colleagues to give you feedback on your body language when you are teaching?
9 How perceptive are you at reading the non-verbal cues that your class give you? For example, can you detect a pupil who is about to do something wrong? Can you pick up easily on the class's mood as they enter the room?

Opportunities

In this section we are going to consider a whole raft of strategies that can be used to create a confident and accomplished impression. It is very important to think carefully about which ones might work for you. One of the critical things in demonstrating confident and effective body language is it needs to look natural and be appropriate to you. Otherwise, it doesn't appear authentic to your pupils. A lack of credibility will really undermine attempts to instil good behaviour strategies. Pupils will see through it, and we will feel awkward. That is not a recipe for being a happy, confident and successful teacher! Think of it as a bit like admiring an item of clothing on a friend. For example, I have a friend who has modelled and is incredibly tall with a completely different colouring to me. The swishy coat looked wonderfully sophisticated, expensive and elegant on her but when I tried it on it drowned me out (I'm five foot three) and made me look like I'd grabbed my Dad's old dressing gown! In the same way, only pick the strategies that make sense and work for you, and make sure that they're strategies that you can confidently 'own'. All the below techniques have worked for *some* teachers in *some* settings.

Setting your dial

This is a useful concept to think about when talking to or teaching pupils. Think about your intention and whether the 'strength' of your non-verbal communication is correct for that situation. I imagine I have a dial, like an old-fashioned cooker dial, positioned in the upper chest region. I think about how much I need to 'turn up the dial' in the given circumstance. The dial relates to how much I project confidence, presence and status. Do I need to increase it? Or would the situation best be served by me turning it down a notch?

We need to think about *how* we 'dial' our non-verbal behaviour cues up or down as appropriate to help our message get through. By this I mean when we talk to some groups of students we might really want to maximise our confidence. For instance, if I am giving a talk to 200 Year 11 students about revision (some of whom might not want to be there) then I will amplify my confident non-verbal signals. How do I do this? I imagine my virtual 'dial' turning up several notches to increase my confidence. Physically, this might involve using more expansive gestures than usual, I might sweep my eyes across the group more often in a slow, confident motion, rather than fixing on one spot, or staring fixedly down. I might use pauses more often to show confidence and let the students really think about what I am saying. Some gestures might be slightly exaggerated for dramatic effect, for example, stopping suddenly if someone in the audience talks, or gesturing more slowly and confidently.

However, if I am working in a lesson with a very small group of Reception children, I will need to dial it down a lot. Otherwise my non-verbal communication will overwhelm and intimidate them. I need to be softer and use more encouraging body language to get the small group to trust me and participate. I am likely to smile and nod much more, especially when working with small groups or working one to one. I will sit at their level. I might use my hand gestures to model what I want the pupils to do in a very obvious and almost exaggerated way. For example, if I want them to listen carefully to each other, I might cock my head on one side, or I might mime putting my finger to my lips in an exaggerated motion to show them that it is time to be quiet now. Many primary teachers will have a raft of really good non-verbal signs that they use to catch the pupils' attention without having to raise their voice. These are often expansive gestures and involve raising their hand or clapping a rhythm to get pupils' attention. In these circumstances, I move my 'virtual' dial up a bit more to catch the attention of the whole group. However, when I need to move closer to a pupil who looks anxious I soften my approach and remove exuberant gestures because they will intimidate. Instead I use softer gestures and a smile as I encourage them to share their work.

On occasion, I have gone between two very different schools in a single day and been too rushed to reset my energy dial before starting with a new group. I have really learnt the importance of setting my dial before each change because if I try to give a talk with my dial set for a small group of primary pupils then I will not be captivating or have a strong enough presence to control the huge group of secondary pupils facing me.

Likewise, if I don't dial it down for the smaller group then I'm likely to come across in a way that is too intimidating. Thinking about this 'dial' is a good way to set your presence correctly and to be mindful of your actions and how they come across. It can be useful to think about how it needs to be set *before* giving an assembly, managing a very robustious bus duty or talking one-to-one with parents. Thinking about your own dial is a good way of checking in with your energy levels and ensuring that they are appropriately matched to what you are trying to achieve with your presence. This is particularly important if you need to switch between teaching seminar style to a small group of grown up sixth formers, and then adapting to 30 rowdy Year 9s or a small primary intervention group of Year 2s.

Research nugget

Amy Cuddy is a psychologist and researcher and has investigated various 'power' poses, exploring how our posture and standing can either increase or decrease our perception of our own levels of confidence. Her poses include standing tall and posing with hands on hips like Superwoman or Superman, or with arms outstretched! Amy's YouTube clips are really worth watching (Cuddy, 2012).

We can make ourselves feel much more confident by how we stand and pose before the pupils enter the lesson. And it is worth doing this before lessons to make us feel more confident – after all, perception is everything! If we feel more confident we will come across as more in control and pupils will respond accordingly. Try a power pose next time you are flagging – but do it before the children see you, and stand normally afterwards – otherwise they might think you are a bit strange...

What do we expect?

It is key to show body language that indicates that you expect the best of pupils and that you are pleased to see them. This sounds obvious but it is surprising how often I see a lesson that isn't going well where it seemed very clear to me (and therefore likely the pupils) that the teacher was not happy to be there. Sometimes it seemed like they did not appear to like the class or even various individuals within that class. Yes, that's right. It was clear *just* from their non-verbal communication. Conversely, if you show controlled but clear positive approaches you will find these are mirrored by the approaches of your pupils and their behaviour.

Do:

- Greet the class by the door (if possible) or confidently face forward in the centre of the space.
- Smile confidently – welcoming them into *your* room with a brief business-like approach. Not an ingratiating smile that seems nervous and uncertain.
- Use expansive arm gestures – by this I mean using the open-handed hand and arm glide. (Think the way the owner of a posh restaurant welcomes you in but expertly guides you to your table.) Positive but in control.
- Speak with your palms facing upwards – this is a positive approach which invites compliance – it is often used in professional speech making and has

a warm open appeal. It draws the listener in. You might use it when you are inviting the class to listen and take certain steps, or when you are introducing something. However, if things are getting a bit tricky you need to change it…

- Use a palm faced down motion if the class are bubbling up and not being respectful and you wish to gain silence. Overusing this palm down approach is more authoritative and can create a rather negative atmosphere though, so use it sparingly.

Owning the room through non-verbal gestures:

- Walking around the room purposefully shows ownership and confidence. For example, opening a window/adjusting a table shows control of the space (you are subconsciously saying *'I'm the boss here, and I welcome you into my domain'*). But try not to pace to and fro as that can be distracting and signal nervous energy.
- Avoiding turning your back on your pupils – even if they are not prone to chucking a missile. Have your key instructions and material readily displayed on the whiteboard. A little mantra I've always had is *'a clicker makes things slicker'* – these handy little presentation clicker pointers are invaluable. They enable you to navigate the screen from any place in the room (without turning your back).
- Stay alert to your pupils by scanning the room. It's natural to want to avoid eye contact when nervous, but briefly meeting each pupil's eyes helps keep them focused and let them know that you 'see' them. Try it in combination with issuing instructions and remember: *sweep don't stare,* as holding eye contact for too long comes across as confrontational.
- Always stand in a specific part of the room to give instructions. Pupils will get used to you standing there and know that you are issuing instructions from that spot.

Using non-verbal strategies to get pupils' attention is a valuable addition to your toolkit. Simply standing still in your usual instruction giving spot with a raised arm will command pupils' attention much more confidently than the steam-engine 'shushing' sound which rarely inspires calm, confidence or authority. By tuning into pupils' non-verbal signals, you will also become more attuned to their understanding, from subtle micro nods, to the looks of comprehension or confusion on their faces.

I see you

Real life cameo

When I was a Head of Department, I mentored a student teacher for the first time. She would be taking over my biddable top set GCSE class. Assuming she would have had behaviour management training at university, I focused on helping her plan a well-structured, engaging lesson to help her feel confident – the class would love her! We talked through each bit of the lesson in small chunks, and of course, I would also be in the lesson so I felt confident it would go well.

Unfortunately, I hadn't anticipated how small aspects of body language could undermine everything. It was a dreary November day and the lesson started. My student teacher stood near the desk, right near the door, wearing a full-length outdoor puffer jacket over her smart work clothes. Unfortunately, she did not remove the outdoor jacket for the entire lesson! She held the resource sheet rigidly in front of her like a barrier and didn't move at all from the small space at the front of the class, as if she was a statue!

The ideas in the lesson were great – but *she did not move at all*. The class were bemused. A girl seated nearest said: *'Miss is she staying?'* 'Of course, why wouldn't she be?' I snapped. 'Well,' she retorted – *'It looks as if she's about to run out of the door!'*

Looking confident is everything, and body language is an essential component of this. I asked my colleague afterwards why she had not moved the *entire* lesson. Her answer: *'I thought if I moved about then they might mess about!'* Pupils need to know that you are in control – and the far reaches of the room hold no fear. We worked on her non-verbal communication, and over time she became a cracking and confident teacher who roamed freely and sometimes even taught from the back of the room!

Dealing with rule breakers and getting things back on track

Be aware of your facial expressions! We want, of course, to try and be genuine, and the best version of ourselves but I sometimes see grimaces, eye-rolling, and other signs of frustration. These might be how we are genuinely feeling in that moment, but try to contain these because they can adversely affect the atmosphere in the lesson and your relationship with the pupils. It is all about being aware and directing our non-verbal communications to good effect. A raised eyebrow, widening of your eyes a slight frown directed at a pupil who is just about to slip chewing gum into their mouth is a good use of non-verbal signs to diffuse a conflict – however a general demeanour of unfocused grumpiness does nobody any good.

When we notice a pupil doing something wrong: opening a packet of sweets, sneaking something out of their bag, moving from their allocated space on the carpet or wearing earrings that break the school rules it is natural to want to tell them off for this, and to ensure that the school rules are adhered to. However, by verbalising what they are doing: *'Ross take your outdoor coat off!'* You are telling the rest of the class that people are *breaking* the rules! Instead of verbalising what you want to happen, first make brief eye contact and mime an action of removing the offending garment. This might sound very strange but trust me it works! Instead of Ross being publicly rebuked in front of his peers (leading to him holding a grudge for the rest of the term) he realises that you have seen him. You are giving him a moment of time to amend his behaviour. When I say 'mime' I'm not talking complex charades, instead its, brief eye contact (so they know they've been spotted) and then indicating a jacket by lightly touching your own top as appropriate. Most pupils know that they are pushing the boundaries and will immediately deal with it. If they don't, then moving closer to them sends the signal that you are coming to deal with it. The best thing about quick mimes is that it doesn't break the flow of the lesson or draw unnecessary action to those who aren't following the rule. Do it with confidence – and it works.

Employing effective non-verbal skills can be a useful tool to start de-escalating situations. It is worth noting how a careful use of our non-verbal skills can help calm situations down. We are always in control of ourselves and our reactions to what happens in the classroom. Whilst moving closer to a pupil who is off-task is a very good way of giving them time to adjust their behaviour – we need to be mindful of being too close to pupils. We are all animals, and if an animal feels cornered, hemmed in or intimidated then they are likely to lash out. Never loom over pupils, point or finger jab or use other body language that could be considered confrontational. Having a few quiet words whilst standing alongside a pupil is less confrontational than facing them head on. Being mindful about this is very important. The phrase *'give them some space'* is a classic for a reason – and often allowing the pupil to 'save face' whilst having the conversation at the end of the lesson or to one side has a more satisfactory conclusion then when they are playing to an audience of their peers.

Finally, if you really need to shift the atmosphere in the lesson consider the movement of pupils. If they won't stop talking – get them all to stand up for a moment – ensure that they are silent and then let them sit down and resume the lesson. Alternatively, getting the class to file out of the room and re-enter silently is a very good way of re-establishing control. It takes time – but it is really worth it.

Once we learn to be aware of our own body language and that of others, we have a remarkable insight into how we influence and improve behaviour. Practise your skill at every opportunity by observing others in day-to-day lessons, in the staff room, on reality tv shows and in the wilds of society. Remember the ability to read situations accurately and influence them appropriately through our non-verbal communication is a massively useful tool in achieving effective behaviour management and diffusing difficult situations.

Way forward

After reading this chapter you might have decided that there are some strategies you would like to trial because you think that they will be useful. Or you might like to observe a member of staff that has good non-verbal communication to see what that looks like in their lessons. You might like to ask a colleague or friend to give you a friendly observation with body language as a focus. Don't try to action too many things at once and remember, adopting new ways of working takes repeated practice, so you might need to keep this focus for a while.

Areas that I think are working well with my classes/individuals are:

_____
_____
_____
_____
_____
_____
_____

Areas I would like to work on relating to non-verbal communication are:

1 _____

2 _____

3 _____

The planned actions I am going to take are:

1 _____

2 _____

3 _____

Review: How did it go? What did I learn? What are my reflections? Am I going to keep any new strategies? Do I have any further steps?

_____
_____
_____
_____
_____
_____
_____
_____
_____
_____
_____
_____
_____
_____
_____

5 The lesson: managing behaviour through high expectations and quality teaching

One of the things that we do have control over with our teaching is the planning and execution of our lessons. The way we design our lessons and how we adapt to changing circumstances (and pupil responses) as the lesson progresses is a crucial part in managing behaviour. In my experience it's one of the most important.

Real life cameo

I am reminded of a pupil I taught who had been permanently excluded from his previous school. As Subject Leader, I was responsible for placing him in a GCSE class. After reviewing a piece of his work, I realised he had a very high ability. But the two Higher Level GCSE classes that had space were taught by a newly qualified teacher (it seemed very unfair to give her a student who had previously been excluded for disruptive reasons), or the previous Head of Department (known for her rigid, combative style). I predicted there would be an inevitable clash and decided to take the pupil on myself.

Though he was frequently removed from lessons by other teachers, he knuckled down in my class. And at the end of the GCSEs, he received the highest coursework grade in the entire year, and outstanding results! Years later he contacted me to tell me that he was now working as a doctor. He had finally realised his potential!

I was due to be running behaviour management training the following day and asked him why he had not misbehaved in my class. His answer

> was enlightening: *'I used to want to mess around in your class – but I never got the chance! And once I realised that I could be good at the subject and you cared about my learning I didn't want to…But initially it was because we never got the opportunity to mess about. You got us learning quickly…'*
>
> Quality lesson planning (removing opportunities to muck about), 'with-it-ness', observing the class and always surveying and moving the class on when necessary is so important for avoiding difficult behaviour. Once quality learning and feedback happens, we can start to see success. A student's self-esteem grows; they start enjoying learning and lessons and the desire to disrupt fades.

Goal: designing lessons that minimise disruption

The careful planning of our lessons can help avoid typical flashpoints and predictable behaviour problems. Having clear and well thought out 'lesson learning' routines helps pupils know where they stand. It can allow them to focus on the learning involved, rather than getting distracted by incidentals – how exactly they should set out their work, or what to do if they have forgotten a piece of equipment.

As an advisor and former inspector, I have observed thousands of lessons across a wide range of schools. It is no surprise to me that the lessons that were effectively planned, suitably engaging and appropriately challenging were the ones *without* difficult behaviour. Or when behaviour started to look like it might become tricky, the classroom teachers were more readily able to resolve it promptly. Furthermore, when we are looking to manage behaviour – we need to remember we are managing behaviour *for* learning. We want lessons to be smooth and have a productive environment. Overall, however, we want great learning to flourish. This is why behaviour *for* learning is important, rather than seeing it as the desire to instil 'good behaviour' itself. We want quality learning that is well managed, not just unswerving compliance. Let's unpick this aim a little further…

When we think of a classroom with great behaviour and great learning we notice several different things that work together to create a harmonious environment. What the teacher or any other adult in the room *does and says* will have a direct impact on the learning in the classroom, as well as explanations and the work that is set. For example, if instructions are not clear or seem overwhelming then confusion will ensue. This confusion leads to off-task behaviour which can escalate if the lesson does not get quickly get back on track.

Great lesson planning means the session can run smoothly and successfully with the outcome that all learners are engaged and learning. The goal in effective lesson planning is to think and plan for what you intend the pupils to learn in the lesson. And to pre-empt and prevent any difficulties that might arise. It sounds so simple!

Planning and adapting lessons

We need to plan very carefully and think about our intended learning for the class *before* the lesson happens. However, a lesson plan is very much like a planned journey – we might meet obstacles and might need to make diversions or pitstops on the way, and that's alright. Sometimes we might not reach our ultimate destination in that single lesson, because we might have had to re-teach something, adapt, give further examples or change the trajectory of our lesson completely. And that is absolutely fine, too.

Doggedly carrying on with a lesson sequence that doesn't suit the needs of the learners doesn't do anyone any favours. A well-planned lesson can help behaviour because you feel confident and knowledgeable about what might come next. Think through the timings, groupings and additional resources needed. Flexibility is also critical here, when we are teaching, we need to be surveying the class with our eyes, looking for any signs of confusion or dismay as this might indicate that pupils are finding the work too tricky or that they don't understand. If this isn't tackled promptly it can easily turn into off-task behaviour as the pupil seeks to mask their lack of understanding or falls into becoming a disruptor.

Planning reinforces our high expectations

The intention should also be that *all* pupils are actively involved in meaningful learning, with tasks designed to challenge and extend every learner so that no pupils are 'sat on the side lines'. Good participation means that there is an increased likelihood of good quality learning, and of course, if pupils are busy learning then they are much less likely to misbehave. A great teacher knows when pupils have mastered something and when it needs revisiting, or when it is time to move on. When pupils are left too long with a task and are actually ready for more this is when poor behaviour starts. Planning smooth transitions between activities will help to avoid disrupting the learning. Lesson time should be well utilised and run smoothly. Finally, end the lessons in a calm way with a reflection or plenary activity that wraps up the lesson and allows pupils to feel that they have made progress and that they are aware of any next steps in learning. Pupils will leave the lesson in a controlled manner, meaning that they are contributing to the purposeful feeling across the whole school. It also enables you to feel emotionally ready to meet the next class or teach the next lesson.

Reality: reflecting on successful lessons

Think about a lesson you have taught recently. Look at the following areas and decide which three you think you are most successful at. Then decide which two you think might benefit from further development. Would your pupils say the same?

You make sure that:

- Lesson planning ensures engagement and focus – pupils are clear are about what they need to do to be successful.
- Lesson planning reflects your high expectations for the class.
- There is clarity on what the pupils are *learning* not just doing.
- You anticipate and plan for what the pupils might find 'tricky'.
- You know your pupils' individual needs and adapting accordingly.
- You use the physical environment to signal high expectations.
- You use 'chunking' for clarity and pupil focus.
- You give clear explanations.
- You keep the lesson fresh with different teaching techniques.
- You achieve 100% pupil participation in lessons.
- You use feedback to motivate, engage, enthuse and inform next steps.

Opportunities: setting a lesson focus and expectations with your class

Lesson planning

All lesson planning should start with a clear focus: what is it we want the learners to know, be able to do and understand as a result? This is critical.

Sometimes we attend training and see an engaging lesson activity or strategy and think '*I'd like to try that. My class would love that!*' That's fine if it helps secure understanding and helps you meet the planned lesson objective. But sometimes it is just an idea that is appropriate in the specific example in the training, (or dare I say it one that just looks fun or captivating) but does not translate to what you are hoping to achieve in your lesson. Always focus on what is it you are hoping to achieve with the learning and then select what might be the best approach to secure this understanding for the learners. I can't emphasise this enough.

It is also important that your ideas for what you hope to achieve are shared with your class (fairly early in the lesson – if not right at the start), and there are two reasons for this. Firstly, some pupils are much more motivated once they see the purpose of what they are being asked to do. If they are asked to do something and it is unclear as to why they should, or it seems a bit strange then they are likely to be resistant. You might get comments like: 'this seems stupid…' or repeated questions of 'why?' This behaviour can start to derail the lesson. As mentioned in Chapter 3, once they know the 'why' then they are more likely to oblige.

Secondly, it shows that you have carefully planned and thought about the lesson – you aren't just making it up on the fly. Presenting yourself like this is one way of showing that through your planning, you are both organised and in control of the lesson's order. Pupils will pick up on this, thinking: '*Miss means business.*' Of course, there's always an exception. Perhaps you are setting up a science experiment, if your lesson objective explains the learning behind it too closely you will give away the whole point of the experiment. Motivation for doing the experiment will therefore drop. Perhaps you want to start the lesson with a speculation? Or get the class to look at a range of equipment and consider what the investigation will be about? Perhaps you want to set up an engaging 'real life' scenario to get them intrigued about the lesson. In examples such as these, explaining the point of the lesson and detailing the lesson objective *initially* might decrease motivation and remove the incentive. In this scenario, it is okay not to share it right at the start, but it is critical that the pupils don't leave the lesson without knowing what they've learnt – rather than just what they've done. For that reason, I'd usually try to explain it within the first twenty minutes or so.

In some lessons, I have observed that the objective is phrased as a big question. This can have several benefits – pupils are not being made to write out long cumbersome learning objectives which can take an enormous amount of time for some (therefore demotivating them before they start learning) and readying them up to display inattentive behaviour. It can also mean that some are too busy trying to copy down the objective so that they miss parts of a crucial explanation which then leads to issues as they don't know what they are supposed to be doing. Big questions can help focus the pupils on the planned learning, as well as motivating them, for example:

'What makes a great persuasive speech?'
'Why did Napoleon lose the Russian Campaign?'
'What do plants need to grow'?

Through pitching the objective as a question, it sparks curiosity, makes the topic relevant to the pupils and you can easily loop back to it towards the end or middle of the lesson to review what has been learned.

When lesson planning it is important to try and pre-empt what might be the challenging parts in the learning for the pupils. Maybe the text you are going to read has some complex or unfamiliar vocabulary that you are not sure that they will understand. You might plan therefore to check this with them beforehand at the start of the lesson. Perhaps writing the meanings on the board or even examine and teach this vocabulary in the lesson before. Even giving them the key words to research or learn in advance of the lesson. By looking at what the potential tricky bits might be – you are more prepared to adapt, flex and head off any obstacles to good learning – thereby preventing difficult behaviour that might have been allowed to sneak in because some disgruntled individuals in the class felt that the learning was out of reach because of their lack of prior learning.

The tricky bits of the lesson might not actually relate to the subject matter. It might relate to the organisation of the pupils themselves – it might be tricky because the pupils are going to need to work in groups and this usually gets them over excited, as they decide who they want to work with. Again, preparation is key here.

Real life cameo

I recently saw a great example of group planning being slickly managed in a Year 5 classroom. The teacher wanted the class to move into groups of four, which might normally spark chatter and debate, but not with this method. At the start of the term the individuals had been given a secondary grouping, for example, famous scientists. She had pre-planned which groupings she wanted before the lesson, so she could readily get them into the groups she wanted without mass discussion and arguments. To make this super-slick she got the students to write their group name in their individual books so they could quickly check if they had forgotten (Newton, Marie Curie etc.). This then meant the organisation was easier as she could just call out: *'All the Newtons move to the table by the door'*. Then pupils would move to sit with their allocated groups without any fuss or confusion.

One sixth form college teacher I know uses tiny animal models – small ladybirds and cats, etc. to help with separating students into groups. At the start of the lesson, she gives these out and students who are given the same animal work together. She acknowledges that it looks random when she gives them out, but she has actually already thought about who she wants to work together for that lesson depending on the requirements of the task set.

Knowing your pupils' individual needs and adapting accordingly

Knowing about any adjustments necessary for accommodating pupils who have SEND is vital to allow you to plan and adapt your lesson accordingly to their requirements, so that they can achieve their full potential. Some of these might be easily put into place *before* the lesson, for example, a pupil who is partially sighted might require worksheets or resources with enlarged text, so these can be pre-prepared. Some adjustments might need to be implemented during the lesson, for example, a student with ADHD might need to be gently redirected when their focus is diverted. Likewise, some pupils with processing issues may need tasks and explanations re-explaining or breaking down further. This is sometimes best done when the others have already started the task when you can circulate and 'work' the room or perhaps by breaking down tasks using mini-whiteboards. Planning a lesson to keep pupils focused is essential. This is where it is important to focus on any areas that might cause difficulty or need adjusting to enable them to be successful with their learning.

Setting high expectations

Whilst we don't want lessons to get derailed because pupils become 'stuck' when the work is too hard for them, it is critical that the lessons are sufficiently challenging. The content we choose to teach also communicates our high expectations for behaviour and effort. Ensuring that the lesson really challenges pupils in a suitable way is so important. Pupils want to feel that they are making progress. If work is too easy it can feel patronising, or as if their teacher doesn't expect anything better from them. This demotivates and where there's demotivation you often get poor behaviour. High expectations are key.

Real life cameo

I observed a Year 9 French lesson where the teacher had told me that the class had struggled with French previously. They had some negative opinions and attitudes towards it, partly because they found it really hard. The teacher had found them very 'difficult' over the first term. He made it his mission to try and not only change their opinion, but to ensure that they made exceptional progress. He realised that he had not been prioritising the planning of their lessons because he felt that they were 'ungrateful' and often complained that things were 'too hard, 'or 'boring' before the lesson got underway.

So, he began to plan their lessons extra carefully and set high expectations. Instead of letting poor pronunciation slip, as he used to, he focused on setting and maintaining high expectations. This included gently but firmly correcting mispronunciations, getting the class members to chorally chant key vocabulary and phrases to build confident and accurate pronunciation, telling the class (truthfully) *'this piece of grammar is something I usually teach at GCSE – but I know you can manage it. So, I'm challenging you with it now!'* He increased praise, not just for accuracy but for positive attitudes towards learning and persistence. He was surprised and thrilled when a huge number of the class selected French at GCSE and had parents tell him that their child had completely changed their attitude towards this subject because of his lessons.

It can seem counterintuitive to set higher expectations when pupils have such an attitude but as long as we give them the necessary support then they can achieve success. Pupils thrive on being appropriately challenged and like to feel that their teacher has the confidence in them to set work that really challenges and pushes their learning. Of course, some might require staging, scaffolding or other adaptions to get them to be able to tackle it successfully – but when they know that you expect great things from them they will rise to that challenge. Showing examples of good work and getting students to unpick its characteristics is also really important. If pupils can understand and see what they are aiming for then they are likely to be more successful.

Physical environment matters

The way we manage our physical classroom and resources helps reinforce our high expectations. I have been in so many classrooms that really promote high expectations effectively. They have displays of pupils' work highlighting what they have achieved. In some secondary classrooms the class teacher has divided up notice boards so that one is for each class that they teach. Sometimes these boards give 'teaser' information about the next topic they will be studying, or they highlight useful terms and ideas for supporting learning connected to the topic. I have even seen pupils actively using these in lessons – putting up their hand to ask to go and 'use the wall' to get ideas about their work or to check things. Some celebrate pupils' work, usually with a notice explaining the context. When I was observing a Year 8 class, one pupil proudly pointed out that his work was *'on the great board'* and told me that he couldn't wait to be taught history in Year 9 too because, as he said, *'just look what they are studying!'* – pointing to a wall with intriguing looking 'historical' information.

I've also seen some inspiring displays that show career pathways and what careers previous students have undertaken after studying a particular subject. These can really pique the interest of pupils as they see what options are open to them after studying in a specific subject. It can help signal higher expectations and this can be particularly important in subjects where they might be perhaps option subjects at GCSE – or ones where pupils cannot always see the direct importance of studying that subject. Additionally, in all these cases the pupils are given another message too, that the teacher has a passion and interest in the subject, and most importantly the teacher wants to ignite their pupils' interest and achievement in it. They notice and it matters. It will help influence better behaviour, because as we know enthusiasm and interest is contagious.

Of course, we don't want pupils to have a sensory overload. Some classrooms with spinning washing lines of information can actually fuel problems as students struggle to concentrate and feel stressed amid too much overwhelm. There is a happy medium. Schools who stop teachers displaying any pupil work or keep all walls blank – even in the corridors – in the hope of keeping student focus on their learning really miss an opportunity to create enthusiasm, interest and celebrate pupil achievement.

Research nugget

One September, a colleague new to the school had a brand-new set of desks for her classroom. She noticed one lesson that a desk had been defaced with graffiti but she didn't get around to getting it cleaned off. She was away for the next week. After she returned, she saw that the graffiti had spread to neighbouring tables and it was a clear issue. Students had seen that others had defaced the tables and so it had spread. Students had also started doodling in the covers of their exercise book too. The 'broken windows' theory, defined in 1982 by social scientists, James Wilson and George Kelling, argues that no matter how rich or poor a neighbourhood, one broken window would soon lead to many more windows being broken 'One unrepaired broken window is a signal that no one cares, and so breaking more windows costs nothing' (Wilson and Kelling, 1982).

While it might sound excessive to link this to pupil behaviour, it is true, we often take our guidance about how to behave from the actions of others. What is accepted or tolerated becomes common behaviour and spreads. It's tough in a busy day to keep on top of organisation but doing so keeps standards of behaviour high, as the pupils notice. In your classroom or any space around school that pupils use (playground, seating area, library corner) pay particular attention to anything that gets damaged or broken. Ensure that any litter, rubbish or equipment is put away carefully after each lesson. Being a stickler for these things – even if they appear inconsequential – will help ensure that expectations are kept high, and this will ultimately reduce the behavioural issues indirectly caused by this.

Explanations

Making sure that our explanations are effective is key in great teaching and helps ensure good behaviour. When pupils are unclear about what they are learning they can feel anxious or unwilling to comply. Misbehaviour becomes one way of deflecting the teacher's and other pupils' attention from their lack of competence in learning. They would rather get told off by poor behaviour than let people know that they can't do whatever is required of them in class. Poor behaviour and a lack of compliance become a defensive mechanism. So, what makes a good explanation?

1. **Clarity:** explain key ideas in short, clear sentences.
2. **Stay focused:** avoid long-winded explanations, unnecessary extra detail or too many contrasting examples. Make sure examples are clear and relevant.
3. **Check vocabulary:** ensure that any new or potential tricky words are checked with the class before teaching. Record them on the board so that they can see the spelling, and if pronunciation is difficult, get the class to repeat it after you.
4. **Keep it digestible:** don't make pupils listen for too long. Break explanations into stages with gaps for pupils to start on the steps so that you aren't giving them too much information all at once.

Ask yourself:

- How you will you get pupils to remember what you have explained? Will there be stages on the board? Will you remind them? Is it an explanation that they will need to remember for another occasion? Do they need to record it?
- What might be the tricky bits or misconceptions? How will you explain these in a way that 'sticks'?
- How will you check in with them to ensure what you hoped that they would understand is secure? Getting pupils to tell you what they think they have understood is a good way of checking.

> ## Research nugget
>
> All teachers (who teach from primary to higher education) I have spoken to since the pandemic have told me that they have noticed that pupil attention spans are much worse now. This comes at a time when there are ever more distractions with technology that feed pupils bite-size videos and tiny snippets of information which they can recall at their fingertips. In their leisure time they often immerse themselves in this immediate gratification of tiny titbits of information. This means they are not used to maintaining concentration with complex tasks or dense information for a sustained period of time.
>
> Researcher, Gloria Mark has been studying attention spans for over 20 years. A 2023 study, presented evidence that attention spans are getting shorter: *'We would shadow people with a stopwatch, and every time they shifted attention, we'd click, 'Stop'. In 2003, we found that attention spans averaged about two-and-a-half minutes on any screen before people switched. In the last five, six years, they're averaging 47 seconds on a screen.'* (Mark, 2023).

Although the above research is focused on concentration when using screens, it's similar to the attention in the classroom – that's why the structure of our lessons is so important in maximising pupils' attention.

Chunking

To maintain pupil interest, it is important to 'chunk' learning into bitesize parts. If we expect pupils to stay in a focused state for very extended periods of time, then we will be disappointed. Some pupils might allow their minds to wander off task and not disrupt the lesson obviously through poor behaviour – but they still won't be learning. Others will show their lack of attention through increasingly disruptive behaviour. Most activities that you do with your class can be easily broken into bite size pieces. For example, planning a suitable introduction, introductory task, development and plenary. Some schools follow the 'I do/we do/you do' approach breaking down the task to firstly illustrate what the class is aiming through teacher explanation and modelling, through to the pupils completing a task on their own. However, even in this structure it can be possible for pupils to become distracted. Breaking down each section further and including questions is a good way of helping pupils' attention and behaviour to stay on track.

Even if you are teaching a lesson whereby the pupils will want to just crack on with the task, for example finishing their piece of art, completing a computer code, or polishing up a piece of drama – it is useful to give them a specific short time allocation. Ensure that you check in with them too – this means it is much more likely that they will stay focused and keep their attention on what you have asked them to do. The fact that you will call them to account by checking in on them and having a 'mini pitstop' when you see how they have been getting on only reinforces this. Explaining to them what you hope that they will have achieved only reinforces your high expectations of them further.

Managing transitions in lessons effectively

An area where things can go askew is when there are transitions between different parts of the lesson. Perhaps they have been focused closely on your explanation but when they are supposed to be working in pairs the noise gets too loud. Or they have been working well independently but you find it tricky to get them all quiet and focused on you. Smooth transitions come from smooth explanations, consistency and ensuring that you don't leave any activity running for an overly long time so that the group has lost focus.

We have already seen the importance of explanations. Think about reinforcing any stages of a task with this noted down on your presentation or board, and don't overload them with unnecessary information. For example, if there are five steps to the work that they are doing which will all have transitions, and it is likely that the most they will get up to is step three in today's lesson then leave step four and five to another lesson. Consistency is your ally in ensuring smooth transitions. It can be helpful to stand in the same place in the room when you issue instructions, for example. Reminding the class of the clear systems for the change of activity, (including the end of the lesson) means a calm transition and mean you stay firmly in control. Avoid the tendency just to want to get the transition going when they are still talking. Always insist on silence.

Lesson ideas: keep it varied, change it regularly

It is important to keep lessons fresh and interesting. Finding new approaches to teaching ideas is key. Imagine if you met up with a friend on a weekly basis, at the same café and she always ordered you the same thing, and told you the same story, in the same way, you'd soon lose interest and crave something different. The same is true for those we teach.

Make sure that you are always on the lookout for fresh ways of teaching things. Share ideas with your colleagues at school and beyond. Social media and online forums offer a plethora of interesting and engaging strategies. There are many advisers and teaching enthusiasts online who share good strategies and recommendations for books and resources about pedagogy. Ensure that you are on the lookout for appropriate CPD both online or face to face. Maintain good links with the person in charge of Teaching and Learning at your school. If you find a particular part of the curriculum or subject area tricky then hone in on this. Most subjects have subject associations. For example: Science has Association for Science Education (ASE) there's the National Association for the Teaching of English (NATE). These produce publications, training and showcase relevant teaching and learning resources.

The more we reflect, try out and secure effective teaching strategies, the higher the levels of engagement there are likely to be in the classroom (and the fewer the behaviour issues). There are also opportunities to observe colleagues teaching a similar class or – if you are in secondary – teaching your class in a different subject area. These opportunities can be particularly enlightening for seeing how teaching impacts on behaviour.

Another opportunity is *Lesson Study*, a professional development process that works in a collaborative way, which was first used in Japan. It encourages teachers to work together in a supportive way to focus on a specific area that they are keen to develop. It includes working as a trio or small group of teachers to focus on developing a particular area of their practice. They co-plan a lesson, trialling out or including strategies that they think will be effective. Then one teacher teaches the lesson, and the other pair observe it in a very supportive way focusing on how the pupils responded to the lesson and how it affected learning. After the lesson, the group debrief and evaluate the approach, before refining and trying the approach with a different group. The focus is on collaboration and support, encouraging colleagues to work with each other to reflect on and develop their classroom practice. It can be a really useful way of getting feedback about things that you are trying out because when you are busy teaching the lesson it can be hard to self-review. We often notice what might appear to have gone wrong in our lesson without noticing the positives. Working alongside a trusted colleague is so useful in developing our teaching prowess which impacts on behaviour.

Get them engaged and wanting to join in

Always plan for total participation when thinking about your lesson – whether that's on the field, in the art studio or in the classroom. Thinking carefully about what each pupil will be doing is key in preventing difficult behaviour. A PE teacher told me that any pupils who were injured or unable to take part in the physical aspect of the lesson were given a clear laminated (re-usable) form of key criteria to look at when observing a practical lesson in a specific sport. So that they could feed back to specific participants about their practice. This not only gave them something relevant to do to keep them focused, but ensured that the pupils who might not be being observed at that moment by the teacher were getting useful feedback about their sporting technique. This also keeps them on task in a helpful way. To enable them to do this in a purposeful manner they were given a laminated A4 tick sheet with the success criteria listed relating to a particular skill. For example, in netball, one of the skills might be: do they pivot successfully? (by managing a controlled pivot, keeping balance and correct footwork?) Do they 'find the space' (moving into areas so that they can receive passes?) Can they intercept effectively (anticipating and stepping in when appropriate)?

Feedback and evaluation

When we give our students useful feedback, we are helping them develop. When we notice what they have done well, when we take time to give them meaningful praise we are building relationships, as well as building better learners. Giving regular feedback 'in the moment' in a busy class, as well as ensuring that any homework or classwork gets appropriate feedback is critical to improving learning and improving relationships. Pupils put renewed effort in if they know that what they are doing is being noticed, valued and appreciated. Of course, feedback needs to feed forward and highlight what they might need to do next to improve but make sure that this is always manageable and that they are clear on what they are aiming for. And always end on a positive.

Way forward

After reading this chapter you will have received some suggestions about high expectations, planning and teaching great lessons. It can be really useful in this area to work alongside a trusted colleague. Activities such as talking through your lesson planning to explain your thinking can be a great way of getting a fresh insight into what's working well, what could be better and how it impacts behaviour.

Areas that I think are working well with my classes/ individuals are:

_____
_____
_____
_____
_____
_____
_____

Areas that I would like to work on relating to setting and maintaining high expectations, aspects of lesson planning and quality teaching:

1 _____

2 _____

3 _____

The planned actions I am going to take are:

1 _____

2 _____

3 _____

Review: How did it go? What did I learn? What are my reflections? Am I going to keep any new strategies? Do I have any further steps? Do I need to seek support/advice from elsewhere?

_____
_____
_____
_____
_____
_____
_____

6 It's all about relationships

'I am the decisive element in my classroom. It is my personal approach that creates climate in the classroom. It is my mood that makes the weather. As a teacher I possess tremendous power to make a child's life miserable or joyous...'

Haim Ginott (1972, P.13).

Teaching is all about relationships. Of course, we have knowledge and skills that we want to pass on to pupils and help them develop. We want to inspire a love of learning and light that fire of curiosity within our charges. But we need to be able to create a calm lesson environment with good behaviour for this to happen. And one of the most important ways for this to happen is through building and developing effective relationships with our pupils, so that the conditions are right for good behaviour to follow. It is only then that great learning will truly flourish.

Goal: building positive relationships

Think for a moment about a really warm, purposeful lesson where pupils work together harmoniously with each other under the guidance of their teacher. This is built upon a strong basis of positive relationships between teacher and pupils, and between pupils and each other. Building good relationships with the pupils in our care, and their parents or carers is the bedrock for fostering a strongly positive classroom with consistently calm, purposeful behaviour. Let's unpick these goals around building relationships.

Can you remember a great teacher you had as a child, or a lecturer at college or university that you greatly admired? What was it that made them so effective? Doubtless you will have remembered them because of their skill in teaching, or the way they breathed life into a subject or topic, making it engaging and memorable. Perhaps you still remember some of their lessons? But I'm sure that their way of building relationships and the atmosphere that they created in their lessons was also a critical part of their success and why you appreciated being taught by them.

We respond instinctively to the actions and intentions of others (those spoken and unspoken). Teachers who manage behaviour successfully know this and maximise this at every opportunity. One of the most wonderful things about being human is our ability to form connections with others. Feeling that we are 'seen', appreciated and understood by others – particularly our teachers – is so motivating.

So how do really effective teachers build relationships with classes and individuals successfully so that pupils really want to behave well, enjoy learning and work hard?

Maslow's hierarchy of needs

Psychologist Abraham Maslow created a pyramid chart to highlight the important needs that people must have to feel fulfilled. It is also a useful insight into understanding human behaviour and motivation and so has much relevance for us today as teachers. If pupils do not have a sense of belonging, for example, which is one of the lower foundations of the triangle, then it will be much harder for them to achieve their potential – or 'self-actualise' and reach their potential higher up the triangle.

Although the diagram is displayed as a triangle – and gives rise to the understanding that one area is baseline and each builds on this, sometimes this is not the case – it might be, for example that one area is fulfilled over another higher level one. I recall the implications of Maslow's hierarchy of needs as a useful reminder that there might be other factors at play when pupils are disaffected or misbehaving. Perhaps they have needs that are not being met? It also helps me think about what I can deal with myself, what I might need to discuss with SLT or refer. It highlights the importance of different areas of pupils' lives.

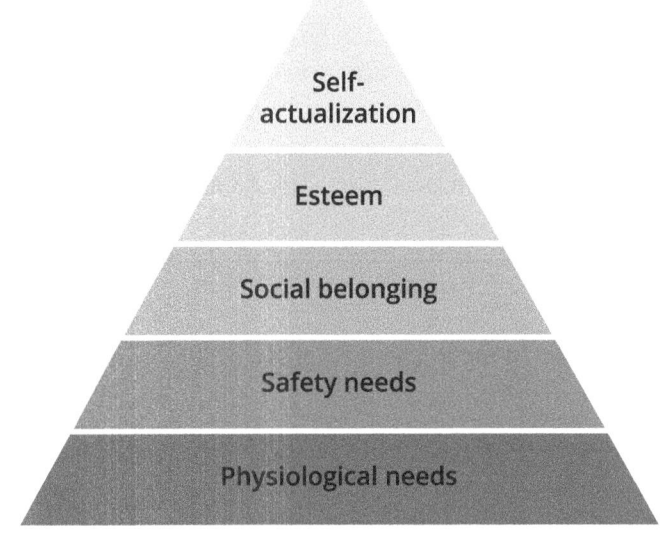

Figure 9: Maslow's hierarchy of needs

On the triangle you will see at the base, **Physiological needs**. These are basic necessities needed for survival, they are crucial and fundamental. When this base is neglected then life is extremely difficult for the young person. We might be teaching pupils who are neglected by their parents, or who are undergoing turmoil related to their housing situation or personal safety or who do not receive regular food or care. Clearly if such basic needs are not being met then their capacity to learn effectively, follow the rules and be in a good mental and physical state for learning will be severely compromised. They might feel like they are operating on the edge, and a harsh word or reprimand can tip them over. Our job is to try and be alert to signs of these so that action can be taken. It is why in primary school the relationship between the class teacher, observant teaching assistant and pupil is so important. In the wider vista of secondary schools, where pupils have many teachers in different subjects, it reminds us of the importance of the form tutor who has that daily 'check in' with pupils and is often the first to notice any signs that all is not well. But an alert and sympathetic class teacher can also notice things and can speak to the form tutor and or the designated safeguarding lead.

I recall a time when I was teaching and came across a situation where a pupil of mine was sleeping on a friends' floor for two weeks because they had been kicked out of their home. We were completely unaware of this and the young person was clearly distracted, distressed and not at their best for learning because their very basic needs were at risk of not being met.

Sometimes the situation is much less serious, but the teacher's reaction can mitigate against making it worse. On a learning walk, I was surprised that during a double maths lesson at 1:45pm a group of about nine boys were seen to be openly munching on their sandwiches and crisps whilst their teacher explained probability. The teacher informed me that the group had been involved in a sporting event and a delay meant they were too late back to get enough time to eat their lunch. She felt that although the school rules strictly forbade eating in class this was one occasion when she would overrule it in the best interests of the pupils. If they were hungry and distracted she thought that very little quality learning would go on, behaviour would worsen and she was right. Popping back at the end of the lesson I saw that they were hard at work – on this occasion the need for strictly observing the rules was less important than ensuring that they weren't hungry and distracted. They appreciated the teacher's empathy and reciprocated by working hard and behaving well.

The next stage of the hierarchy is **Safety needs**. We know that pupils need to be physically safe and the environment needs to be free from literal dangers – whatever they might be. However, it also refers to psychological safety.

How do we as educators ensure that pupils feel 'safe' so that they are happy to join in activities and they don't feel ridiculed? They should feel that they can share their ideas confident that they will be appreciated. This is all critical for good learning and deterring difficult behaviour. If they feel unsafe then this is when pupils can either lash out or try and shrink away from participating or even attending lessons. What creates the safety in lessons is the way the teacher fosters a psychologically safe environment: the way we respond to pupils, how we set out ground rules for discussion and have no tolerance for pupils behaving unkindly towards each other. This is often best done by modelling what respectful behaviour to others looks like and by clamping down swiftly on any classroom behaviours that threaten any other students' safety needs. It is also about being thoughtful about the pairings and groupings in the classroom so that pupils are not grouped with those that they might clash with.

Next is **Social belonging** which is one of the most critical needs. And it is one that teachers can easily foster. How do we create the sense of belonging in the classroom? Do pupils feel welcomed, greeted (at the door), do they feel that their contributions are valued and that they are appreciated and their presence is respected?

I hope you have never have had the experience of not belonging, but it can be a very unpleasant and isolating experience even for a very short time. It can lead to low self-esteem and pupils not wanting to participate in classroom activities. There is a lot we can do, however, to create a sense of belonging. Being aware that the rest of the class will take their guidance from us and how we respond to pupils is critical. We must never ridicule pupils, or leave some out, in order to gain approval from others. We need to be clear that we will not tolerate unkindness or bullying or mocking of each other. It is these behaviours that create seething resentment and angry outbursts by some pupils when they feel excluded, resentful and that they do not belong.

Some pupils will find learning easier than others; some will be more popular or obviously more likeable than others. Some might struggle with what we ask them to do and will need more guidance, cajoling and support. But it is our place to make the classroom a warm and enabling place for all and we do that by our behaviours and by seeing pupils as individuals. Greeting at the door is one way of welcoming them and it also reinforces good behaviour as you show that you are 'on it', for example, you can say briskly, 'tuck your shirt in'. It sets the lesson off in a purposeful way with them under your warm, but firm, direction.

Esteem relates to pupils having a feeling of accomplishment and self-worth through achievement. One of the best ways of increasing pupil motivation is for them to see that they *can* achieve, and that progress is possible. Here careful task setting, guidance and support (when necessary) is the way that this can be accomplished. Everyone needs to have a healthy self-esteem. Giving clear feedback, praise and letting them know that they are making progress is critical here. Some pupils really struggle with parts of the curriculum, and it is essential that quick 'wins' are built in and that they can feel that they are making progress and headway even if it is very incremental. Our self-esteem is linked to how much effort and energy we will give a task, or whether we feel that it is totally beyond our reach. Careful lesson planning, feedback and praise are fundamental to ensuring that esteem is maintained by students.

At the top of the pyramid is **Self-actualisation** where the individual feels that they are realising their potential as a person, and of course academically and socially at school and in wider life. When one feels that they are fulfilled then anti-social behaviour is much less likely to occur.

Reality: your relationship with your pupils

Let's explore your reality in the area of relationships. For each of the following statements decide on your score for each one, with five as completely the case through to zero (not at all). Then review each area to see where in the opportunities section you can find suggestions that might help you develop in this area.

A) How good are you at using pupils' names?

0	1	2	3	4	5

B) Do you take an interest in pupils' achievements outside of school? (e.g. sports and hobbies)

0	1	2	3	4	5

C) Do you frequently give praise – verbally and by using the school systems?

0	1	2	3	4	5

D) Do you give descriptive praise, explaining <u>exactly</u> what it is that pupil has done well?

0   1   2   3   4   5

E) Do you notice and acknowledge pupils' improvements (rather than just praising achievement and excellence)?

0   1   2   3   4   5

F) Do you contact pupils' parents/carers to relay good news?

0   1   2   3   4   5

G) Do you always make time to listen as well as to talk?

0   1   2   3   4   5

H) Do you have strategies to deal with pupils who don't settle to their learning quickly?

0   1   2   3   4   5

I) If you tell your pupils that you are going to do something do you always follow through?

0   1   2   3   4   5

J) Do you have effective strategies for supportively dealing with pupils who haven't started a task?

0   1   2   3   4   5

K) Do you have good awareness of yourself and how you regulate your emotions in a lesson?

0   1   2   3   4   5

L) Do you supportively help pupils challenge negative assumptions they have about themselves?

0   1   2   3   4   5

M) Do you create a warm, purposeful learning climate where pupils feel that they can give a hard task a go?

0   1   2   3   4   5

Opportunities: building positive foundations

Here are **eight foundations** of building relationships with your class:

1   Create a sense of belonging

Pupils, like all humans, naturally seek a sense of belonging and connection, they are looking for their 'pack'. They look for signs of approval and acceptance. One of the reasons that gang culture can seem so attractive to young people is because gangs build strong connections and a sense of community. Individuals feel noticed and accepted. This is a very attractive combination particularly for those students who sadly lack positive adult interest or attention at home and feel adrift socially and emotionally.

Teachers who effectively build strong relationships with their class have mastered creating the feeling of belonging. A feeling of being part of a collective, purposeful group. This fosters positivity and wellbeing for all. One strategy for doing this is learning pupils' names quickly and using them frequently. When someone learns our name and pronounces it correctly, this creates a feeling of warmth and belonging. We feel 'seen' and effort has been made to notice us. We feel that we matter. Salespeople know this well and it is one of the top tips that is used in sales seminars: use the customer's name early, frequently and correctly.

It creates a bond. We feel noticed and in return we want to please, whether that is by participating in class or being much more tolerant to listening to the salesperson's pitch.

Moreover, someone who remembers and uses our name appears much more 'on it'. They present as someone who is proactive, organised and certainly not a push-over in the business world or the classroom. Whether it's the salesperson who remembers that you always like to book a beach holiday every year for your anniversary or the teacher who always uses your name and remembers that you were trying out for the hockey team at the weekend. We know that teachers who are 'on it' and who look proactive and alert are much less likely to have pupils who will take the chance to mess around in their lessons. These all convey the message that the person *cares*. With teachers we *know* that relationships matter, we want our pupils to thrive, achieve and grow. We use pupils' names to foster belonging and we do it because the pupils count and this is one simple way of demonstrating this.

Real life cameo

A supply teacher told me that her use of pupils' names is a key reason behind her success and management of behaviour. Her top tip: *'I make sure when first completing the register to try and get pupils' names right. I ask them to tell me if any pronunciations are incorrect. I make a real effort. Or if they have any preferences with shortenings of their name – if Alexander always likes his full name used then shortening it to 'Alex' can feel like a forced familiarity. It really fosters good relationships. I tell them – please correct me if I get it wrong.'* The class really appreciate her efforts, and the school tells me that she is the most respected and requested supply teacher.

My neighbour persistently calls me 'Carolyn' despite me having corrected him for the last eight years, so I can certainly attest to how not using the correct name feels really frustrating! It's just one strategy but knowing names and using them correctly and frequently matters when building relationships. Don't feel ashamed to rely on a seating plan to aid you at first. If pupils see you struggling but making the effort to learn their names, they will really appreciate it. Directly addressing a child by name gives you much more authority than giving vague instructions to *'you at the back.'* It helps you pinpoint exactly who you are talking to. This will give you confidence and help with control. Pupils will see that you are 'on it'!

2 Take an interest

Everybody wants to know that they matter to their teacher and that their teacher is interested in their progress and sees them as an individual. When things are difficult with a class it can feel that they are just a 'mass' of group negativity directed at you. This is why viewing the class as unique individuals really matters and will influence their behaviour for the better.

> ### Real life cameo
>
> Upon starting at a new school, the Year 10 form group (all boys) I inherited were grumpy, borderline rude and very resentful of me as their new form tutor. They sighed and I felt a collective animosity from them directed towards me at every interaction. Tutor time was painful and hostile. They delighted in telling me that their previous form tutor was *'amazing'*, and I got extremely fed up of hearing how wonderful he was. In fact, I had to bite my tongue on several occasions from saying, *'Well he obviously didn't think the same about you – because he left!'* (Thankfully I remembered the golden rules of behaviour – don't take things personally and of course, *always* be professional). Their behaviour was getting worse, not better, over the term. My kind and insightful Head of Year gave me some seemingly strange advice. He told me that at lunchtime the form were playing a rugby match; I should definitely go and watch them. I could think of nothing worse! It was October; the field would be wet and boggy. I had lots of marking to do and frankly could have done with a proper break over lunch. However, he took no excuses and directed me towards a pair of neglected wellington boots that were far too small for me. So, at lunchtime I stood huddled, unsteady and resentful in the muddy field watching the group run about after a ball. I was not happy and felt it was a waste of my time. None of them even acknowledged me on the side lines.
>
> I was so surprised by the quiet in the form room after lunch. One of the most troublesome boys spoke up and said: *'You came to watch us play'* in a surprised voice and a constructive conversation about the match (which they had apparently won) took place. From then on I sensed a thawing towards me and behaviour, whilst by no means perfect at first, drastically improved. I attended other events (more happily), and a truce was formed. I soon saw them as individuals with different strengths and

> interests rather than an unruly group. They in turn they accepted me as their new tutor. Standards of behaviour improved, and they came to me with their concerns about school and life. All because I made an effort to take interest in them outside of lessons.

3 Use plenty of praise

Praise has had an undeservedly poor reputation as a behavioural tactic over the years. One teacher told me that he 'didn't believe in it' and pupils should just automatically give their best and behave. Unsurprisingly he had issues with classroom management as the class picked up on his negativity. Feedback and giving clear points for development clearly is, of course, the strategy that leads to improvement in pupils' academic work. However, it is meaningful and frequent praise helps to oil the classroom relationship wheels and build positive behaviour in the long term.

A good use of praise is noticing when pupils as individuals and groups have done something particularly well or have made a good effort. It is crucially important that effort is noted and appreciated because trying hard and using strategies are mindsets that we really want to encourage. Giving praise just for top scores and 'easy' excellence doesn't value often the higher effort of those that persevere. We really want to foster 'growth mindset' whereby pupils can see that they have the option to improve their work through applying effort and reflection.

Research nugget

Research has demonstrated that having the mindset that you are either 'smart' or 'not smart' has serious negative consequences for learning. Fortunately, one powerful way that you can intervene as a teacher is by being careful about how you give students praise. Offering praise for students' work and efforts can alter this mindset so that students can begin to view their own intelligence as something that can be developed. This mindset of developing intelligence will increase students' ability to 'bounce back' in the face of academic setbacks and other difficulties (Dwyer, 2006).

The best praise is very specific. Praise that is clear, directive and explanatory is valued much more than just a 'well done'. Use the pupil's name or highlight the group's collective effort. *'Well done group 2 I can see you've all have made a great effort to...'* Sometimes some very 'peer conscious' pupils appear not to like being singled out for praise. This is where highlighting the 'group' that they are in for praise can be useful. Although, I would argue that everybody really likes praise (even if they don't admit it), and we need to aim for a classroom where praise can be readily given by us but also from peer to peer. For example, when work is shared with the class, asking another pupil to comment on something that their partner did successfully.

Sometimes with a very difficult class it can seem impossible to find anything to praise. They might *all* appear to be misbehaving and not following instructions. However, by pointing out and mentioning those that are doing what you want you will find that more start to behave. However, if you just point out what some are doing wrong – really highlighting this to the group – you are effectively telling them that the opportunity to mess around does exist.

Research nugget

Research highlights the transformative impact of praise across a variety of contexts. In a 1995 study carried out by Hart and Risley, they identified that offering five approvals for every one disapproval improved behaviour results (Flora, 2000, p.64-69).

Can you challenge yourself to up the praise in your interactions and lessons? Notice what happens when you do.

Use the school or college system for praise and think of additional ways that you can reward students through giving praise or recognition. I recently led a training session at a sixth form college and I was impressed by one teacher's system. On the wall were three laminated A4 sheets with clear titles such as, **'Student question of the week'** and **'Work of the week'**. It was clear that when a student gave a good answer in this area their name was captured and displayed for the week. What a positive way to highlight excellence, improve everyone's knowledge and weave in praise! It is important that the rewards are genuinely given otherwise they will not be valued and students will stop appreciating them. Celebrating their work on walls is one way of very publicly rewarding this.

The classroom environment can be a very public and powerful way of enhancing relationships. Pupils who have their work displayed on the wall as examples of excellence will really appreciate it. A secondary colleague divides up the display boards per class – and uses them to create a sense of interest and awe about the area that they are studying. Sometimes the board will pique their interest about a new topic they are studying. But, she also uses it to display effective work – ensuring that all pupils get a chance to shine. For example, she created an effective display about story writing using different famous novel openings – alongside carefully crafted student openings. These made for an interesting an interactive display and students were thrilled to see their great story openings alongside some famous authors.

Praise 'up the chain' too. Letting parents and carers know of their child's achievements is a key aspect in developing and strengthening relationships. Some parents have told me they fear picking up the phone in case it is the school telling them that their child has been misbehaving again. Sometimes the only interaction they have from the school that month is a negative one, and it can sometime seem like the teachers' stress is being offloaded onto them. I distinctly remember one mother crying on the phone when I telephoned to tell her that her child (a boy who had been excluded from another school) had completed a fantastic piece of work – she was waiting for the 'but…' There was no 'but' in that phone call and this really strengthened our relationship. The parents knew I wanted the best for him. Of course, there were other less congratulatory phone calls in later months, but that positive relationship had been created. All relationships are an exchange of either information or emotion, and when you have these positive exchanges it makes a deposit into 'bank' of parental goodwill. So that when you might need to raise an issue or explain a tricky situation there is already some goodwill there. Making contact with home can seem time consuming and it is tempting to let 'no news' be good news. However, using whatever school rewards systems there are, or picking up the phone or writing an email is so important to helping smooth relations and to help foster good relations with pupils and parents too.

4   Listen and follow through

As a teacher we are most often the ones talking. Listening is an underrated skill and in building relationships with pupils, it is critical to listen carefully. It is important to get to the heart of why things are going askew when behaviours and attitudes are 'off' by ensuring that we listen and the pupil feels heard. All too often I have seen staff jump down the throat of a pupil who was misbehaving, when listening and asking a few insightful questions might have resolved the issue. We can increase the tension and worsen behaviour by immediately leaping in. When a pupil hasn't started their work, do we quickly zoom in on them? Do we ask them 'why' they haven't started yet? Or do we give them a minute or two to think about the task? We might ask an open question giving them the opportunity to explain whether they understand the task or not. It can diffuse tension. Thinking about the words we use is important. Asking 'why?' can feel very loaded especially when discussing behaviour. None of us respond well to the *'why did you do that?'* Whereas *'can you explain…?'* or *'I'm curious about...?'* creates a less of confrontational tone and is more likely to get a positive response.

5   Support them

Why aren't they on task? It is important to ascertain if pupils aren't working (after some take up time) because they are unclear on the task, or because they are 'stuck' and might need some further support or guidance or because they are just trying to avoid the task. Asking open questions and checking in with them is important to judge next steps. Being given a blank sheet of paper and asked to start writing can feel quite alarming to some pupils and this can then cause difficult behaviour.

For many students, the approval and respect of their peers is much more critical than that of their teachers. They would rather 'kick off' or maintain task avoidance, rather than lose face with their peers and been seen to admit that they don't know what to do, or even worse that they can't do it. Carefully finding out whether they 'can't' or 'won't' is key. Giving sentence openers, some strategies or suggestions, or even just talking about their approach can head off distracted behaviour that is caused by pupils struggling with the demand of the work. Knowing when to do so is an important part of reading the situation. Useful scaffolding and supportive measures can really help 'get pupils going', but of course we don't want to offer too much support if it is not required as this will reduce challenge and good learning. Creating a supportive culture in the classroom is key – as is asking: *'What questions do you have?'* when setting a task – rather than: *'Do you have any questions?'* The former encourages pupils to seek clarification and stops them heading off down the wrong path. The implication of *'do you have any questions'* in many classrooms is that the answer should be: 'no'. And this is sometimes where the difficulties start. Slight alterations in the way we say things can create a much more supportive arena and give fewer opportunities for pupils to say: *'I didn't know what I was supposed to be doing'* thereby avoiding giving them the opportunity to misbehave.

6 Be reliable and create a sense of trust

Let your class know that you want the best for them through your actions. When they have concerns or worries try and help them find a solution. When pupils know that you genuinely want the best for them and that you will do what you say you will it nurtures the relationship and creates that sense of trust. Pupils will then want to please you and this will lead to them aspiring to better behaviour. If we say that we will speak to their PE teacher, read over their application for a part time job or watch them perform in a House competition then following through really matters.

7 Be aware of yourself

Having an accurate awareness of yourself, and your own contribution to the atmosphere in the classroom, is crucial. Think back to Haim's quote at the start of this chapter, and the well-known phrase: *'You create the weather in your classroom.'* It is really so true. Being in tune with your own emotions, feelings and stresses is important. If we let some of them subconsciously slip through to the pupils we teach then this can affect the behaviour negatively. Deliberately and carefully raising an eyebrow at a pupil who is about to do something wrong, or deliberately looking unhappy at an action a pupil is about to do is one thing. These are carefully planned responses designed to tell pupils in a non-verbal fashion that you are unhappy with what they are about to do. They prevent poor behaviour. However, when we unconsciously let our personal frustrations, fears and foibles leak out this is very different.

One of my teacher friends, when she feels that she's becoming a bit tense or can feel her annoyance rising, always gives the class something to focus on and respond to so that she can have a minute to re-centre herself. A good example is saying: *'turn and talk to the person next to you about x for a minute'*. Pupils are engaged and focused as the turn and talk is always centred on the lesson material, and she gets a moment to refocus and recalibrate. Pupils also get that moment to let off steam in a positive way by discussing the question or statement that has been posed. We must be aware of our 'own weather' and the effect that it can have in the classroom. By modelling the sort of behaviour we would like to see in the classroom and showing our best side to the pupils, we are modelling the sort of behaviour we would like to see in return. It sets an achievable expectation of high standards of behaviour.

8   Help develop pupils' skills in managing their behaviour

When young people are angry or their feelings are hurt it can feel (to them) like the world is out to get them. Hurt and angry youngsters often talk in absolutes. They say things like: *'I'm rubbish at everything,'* or *'all the teachers hate me,'* or, *'I don't see the point of bothering in maths – I'm still rubbish at it.'* Often these are smoke screens designed to hide their fear of not doing very well, their fear that they have got a 'bad' name in the school, or their worry that even if they did try it could still all go wrong. By building relationships with them and gently helping them see that their reactions aren't helpful, we can help them see that there are things that they can do to change up their situation. Often, they feel that they lack power to make the changes themselves.

> ### Real life cameo
>
> I observed a skilful Head of Year discussing the behaviour of a boy who was very down on himself and school. He was in trouble. When he insistently mentioned that he was *'Not good at anything,'* the Head of Year gently, but persistently challenged this. Asking him: *'Are you sure? Not anything at all? What about History? I hear you were doing well at History.'* *'Oh well,'* the boy admitted, and by discussing this gleam of positivity and breaking down the absolutes the teacher started discussing what the pupil could do to work on improving the other areas. This was only possible because of the strong relationship they had formed. Respectfully challenging assumptions and helping pupils reflect is an important part of building relationships.

Way forward

After reading this chapter you will have received some suggestions about relationships. It is worth looking at your interactions with pupils with fresh eyes. What's working well? What could be better? If you work in secondary or at college then there will be other staff teaching these students. How might observing or talking to these staff about their experiences increase your knowledge? What can you learn from them?

Areas that I think are working well with my classes/individuals are:

_____
_____
_____
_____
_____
_____
_____

Areas I would like to work on relating to relationships are:

1 _____

2 _____

3 _____

The planned actions I am going to take are:

1 _____

2 _____

3 _____

Review: How did it go? What did I learn? What are my reflections? Am I going to keep any new strategies? Do I have any further steps? Do I need to seek support/advice from elsewhere?

_____
_____
_____
_____
_____
_____

7 Voice control: the importance of what you say and how you say it

Your voice is your essential tool when teaching. Giving clear and accurate instruction and effective explanation relies on using your voice well - but it's so much more. Although we use our voice all the time, this is an area that is often neglected in initial teacher training and in future training Inset sessions, when really it needs revisiting. There are certain things that we can learn and use that really make the difference. Use and protect your voice well and you are on the way to managing behaviour smoothly and successfully. Fail to use it effectively and you can end up screeching, looking like you've lost control, and it can damage your vocal cords, as well as your relationship with your class!

Using your voice effectively is crucial for influencing behaviour. We also want to regulate the voices of our pupils so that classrooms have a pleasant buzz of activity, rather than sounding like noisy disordered places. Ensuring that we can gain pupils' attention and get them quiet quickly with minimum stress is also central in managing behaviour. It also makes transitions between part of lessons much smoother. In this chapter, we will consider the physical use of our voice, (how to use it and protect it) but also the words and choices that we make when we talk to our pupils. These are critical in enthusing pupils, refocusing them and keeping them on track. We will also look at successful ways to moderate our learners' voices – as excessive noise can be a real issue and concern for many teachers. We will unpick the best ways to get pupils focused and listening to us and each other – without shouting!

Everybody wants to have their voice heard – pupils and teachers. Allowing for active engagement with the learning is a good way to do this, and it helps keep pupils motivated.

> **Real life cameo**
>
> A teacher told me about an experience he'd had on an Inset training day: There was a whole day of different workshops with experts, and they were all about topics that were relevant to him. Each trainer spoke for about an hour and although each individual topic was interesting, the teachers didn't get to interact at all. There wasn't even time for questions at the end. After the second 50 minutes of having to sit and listen, the teacher was bursting to speak to his neighbour, or to anyone! He also noticed that throughout the day low level off-task behaviour was happening *everywhere* – and these were motivated, professional adults! People were shifting in their seats, checking their phones, getting distracted, whispering to each other, going late to the next session. This teacher really lost interest after the first session. It made him think about how sometimes teachers insist on pupils being silent for far too long. This is unrealistic and undesirable, without the opportunity to participate in a positive way, they bubble over and behaviour declines. Pupils need to hear their own voices too, as much as we want them to listen to ours.

Goal: choosing the right words and using your voice

We are going to unpick what it would be like to be great at using our voice and using effective verbal communication. First, let's consider our actual physical voices. This includes how our voice sounds, the tone and pitch that we use and how we actually speak to ensure that pupils receive our message clearly and feel motivated to act on it.

> **Research nugget**
>
> The University of Glasgow and Université Aix-Marseille investigated how listeners form impressions of a person just from how they uttered a word, using different intonations, pitch or tones. They found that impressions were consistent across a range of listeners! (McAleer, Mahrholz and Belin, 2017) Emotions and feelings in pupils can also be generated by the way we use intonation, pitch and pace.

Our voice is one of our most personal features. It's part of us and how we present ourselves to the world. If we receive criticism about our voice, it can feel very upsetting. During online training once, a teacher revealed that a Senior Leader observing his lesson had said that *'his voice wasn't good at all.'* As the teacher revealed this, it was clear by his facial expression that he was absolutely crushed by this unhelpfully vague, negative comment. And who can blame him! I'm sure that the reviewer didn't mean it to come across like this, but the generally *unhelpful* and critical comment was absolutely devasting to the teacher's confidence.

While our voice is very personal, we still need to make sure that it's the best it can be. We need to use it to motivate pupils and ensure clarity in giving instructions. We also need to avoid excessive strain that might create future vocal issues.

Interesting nugget

What does your own voice sound like?

It can be shocking when we hear a recording of our voice – because it sounds completely different to what we expect. I asked a doctor friend of mine for an explanation. He reminded me that when we listen to speech our ear drums vibrate and transmit vibrations to the inner ear. There is a damping effect because of this and so not all frequencies are heard evenly. When we talk, and hear ourselves speak, sound is transmitted as described but also through direct vibration of the skull and therefore the inner ear. This energy transmission is perceived as a somewhat different tone. So, now you know why you sound different on a recording!

Making your voice work for you!

Think about a famous actor or celebrity whose voice you really like. What is it about their voice that you enjoy?

I imagine that my choice might not be the same as yours. But from asking a wide range of people, although they prefer different people's voices, unsurprisingly they often choose actors who will have had formal voice training, the reasons they give for their choice are all similar. The voices that are preferred are often low and melodious, rather than high pitched and squeaky. They have warmth in them, and some range and texture; by this I mean that they vary their tone and pace. They sound more happy or positive than melancholic. They might also have a regional accent that provokes positive connotations. Apparently, many call centres have recruited people with a Scottish or Yorkshire accent as they are popular to listen to, and many people associate them with warmth and honesty!

On the other hand, I'm sure you can think of circumstances when the way somebody has spoken to you has really frustrated you. Some words and phrases are likely to be inflammatory, for example, if somebody starts a statement telling you: *'I don't mean to be rude but…'*, you know the next statement is definitely going to be judgemental with a side of unpleasant! But here I'm thinking about the *way* someone sounds and *how* they use their tone of voice. Voices that are overly loud and hectoring, ones that don't pause for breath or that are very abrupt are all off putting and, most importantly, can inflame an already tricky situation.

The importance of tone of voice

There are various components that make up your voice which include **tone**. The Cambridge dictionary describes tone as: *'a quality in the voice, especially one that expresses the speaker's feelings, often towards the person being addressed.'* (Cambridge University Press, 2025). This highlights the critical nature of tone because those that are listening will pick up on our attitudes and feelings towards them by the way that we speak. Tone is *so* important because it can be detected – even when the individual words aren't always heard clearly!

Real life cameo

When visiting a friend, I could hear her husband in the kitchen (behind a closed door) having a conversation with a neighbour; I could tell by the tone of the husband's voice and the loud, hectoring tone of the neighbour that things weren't go well. The neighbour's voice was loud, but their tone was strained and persistent. I could tell that he was under stress, but belligerent even though I couldn't hear what he was saying. When my friend explained that the neighbour had caused damage to their garden, it made sense – my friend didn't need to follow up that the neighbour was being difficult and refusing to accept responsibility. I could hear it in the angry tone, the lack of pauses and the volume – the sound of tension was radiating through the door.

Think about your tone of voice. How would you like to sound? What mood do you want to communicate to your class when you are explaining something? Look at the **tone box** below and think about the different types of tone there are. Which would you like to use in different circumstances? When would you want to use an alternate tone? Are you aware of when you alter and adapt your tone? Are you aware of how the use of tone contributes towards the successful management of behaviour?

Adjectives to describe your voice: how would you like to sound?

Happy, compassionate, joyful, sympathetic, annoyed, reassuring, respectful, serious, stern, vibrant, optimistic, enthusiastic, thoughtful, excited, friendly, gentle, concerned, soothing, encouraging, calm, encouraging, playful, uplifting, firm, sincere, motivational, commanding, inspiring, gentle, vibrant, supportive, crisp, humorous, warm, cheerful, gentle, confident, light-hearted, uplifting, authoritative, respectful, polished, serious, laid-back, approachable, lively, assured, dramatic, passionate, conversational, dynamic.

Tone matters!

Pupils are much more likely to listen to us if we vary our tone. Imagine if we always spoke like a hyped-up children's tv presenter or tv game show host, bubbly, upbeat, ridiculous enthusiasm *constantly* – it would wear thin after a very short time. Likewise, the droning monotone is never a good choice in any situation. We need to catch the interest of pupils if we want them to give their attention to us. Having an enthusiastic tone is important because enthusiasm is contagious. If we show that we are pleased and eager to teach our class and to start and explain a task then it is much more likely that they will give it a go too and any potential behaviour problems are nipped in the bud. You can see this in action in lessons and it's brilliant to observe.

But it is important to have light and shade in our voice. Keeping our voice varied makes it interesting and allows us to give emphasis to important things. It is also essential to be aware of when we are letting our true feelings show through our tone when perhaps they could be more professionally concealed. For example, I once attended a staff meeting with a school after they had had a Local Authority review that had highlighted some key issues that needed to be improved. Although there were important issues to address, they were fully resolvable, but unfortunately the Headteacher's extremely weary and pessimistic tone to his staff in a briefing designed to motivate them and plan out their actions communicated a completely different story to his words. Even though he was making encouraging statements, the tone, coupled with big sighs, highlighted to the staff that he didn't really feel that they could improve, and he simply didn't have the resolve to follow through on things. A palpable mood of depression and despondency settled over everyone very quickly because his tone told them that he lacked confidence and it was all too much. What we say certainly matters – but *how* we say it often matters much more. Our word choice and tone need to match, otherwise people soon realise that we do not mean what we say – and they lose trust in us.

Have a go…

Try reading these words in a neutral tone:

money, credit card bill, Taylor Swift tickets, bubonic plague, traffic jam, lottery win, new puppy

Then repeat them and play around with the tone: joyful, excited, secretive, humorous, despairing. Can you hear how important the tone of voice is in conveying meaning rather than the word itself?

Those that manage behaviour effectively are usually great at managing their voice. They use it to engage their class effortlessly and use range and the tone that is most suited to their purpose. Great behaviour managers also know that they need to use the volume of their voice carefully. They know that raising their voice loudly will raise the base level sound of the classroom with the result that *everyone* will get louder until it is impossible to hear yourself.

We all know that shouting causes strain and gives the impression of a lack of control. This is also transparent to the pupils we teach. When I asked some GCSE students about the biggest mistakes teachers made when trying to manage behaviour this came up time and time again as one of the worst flaws: *'many shout too much or try to always be super loud – it's often better to just talk and make everyone quiet that way.'* Paradoxically dropping your voice lower – after first initially attracting the pupils' attention will result in pupils listening more carefully, as they must make the effort to hear what is being said. We know that shouting needs to be reserved for the rare urgent action, such as alerting pupils to the unexpected potentially dangerous situation – rather than as a form of regular management control or a casual rebuke.

Reality: let's get real!

In this section we are going to raise some questions about the use of your voice. These are all key in keeping your voice working effectively and allowing you to manage behaviour competently. Below are a range of statements linked to our use of our voice and the words and phrases we use. Look at each statement and give it a traffic light code to show whether you feel confident about each of them (green), it's something to work on (amber), or it's not there yet (red).

Don't worry if you end up with many red or amber sections as we will unpick how to change these to green later in the chapter.

Let's talk about it: what's your reality?

1. I know how to 'warm up' my voice before my lessons, so that I am protecting it and getting the best out of it.

   Red
   Amber
   Green

2. When I speak in front of the class I try and keep my body in a relaxed state, and let the sound make the effort.

   Red
   Amber
   Green

3. When I need to get the class's attention, I don't strain my voice or shout. I manage to get their attention quickly.

   Red
   Amber
   Green

4. I know how to take care of my voice. For example, I sip water regularly and rest my voice if I am unwell. I seek medical advice if I have any concerns.

   Red
   Amber
   Green

5 I have a range of tone and vary it deliberately in lessons, conscious of the effect it has on others.

Red
Amber
Green

6 I often 'check in' on how I sound in lessons and how the pupils are responding.

Red
Amber
Green

7 I speak at an appropriate speed. I don't gabble or speed up if I feel nervous.

Red
Amber
Green

8 I try not to let frustration show in my voice – unless I am doing it for a very deliberate effect.

Red
Amber
Green

9 I allow my pupils to hear their voices in the lesson, and this is managed in a controlled manner. This is purposeful and it contributes well to the learning in the lesson.

Red
Amber
Green

10 I have some useful strategies for managing questions and class discussions so that when pupils talk it is controlled and productive.

Red
Amber
Green

11 I have strategies to ensure that a good range of pupils participate in each lesson.

Red
Amber
Green

12 I've asked a friend or colleague to give me feedback about how I use my voice. I am aware of any vocal habits I have that can be distracting to pupils.

Red
Amber
Green

Have a look at the statements where you are red or amber. Do you notice anything particular about them? The Opportunities section below provides pointers to help you develop in these areas.

Opportunities: taking care of your voice and body

In this section we are going to consider what we can put in our vocal toolkit to help us be the best we can. It is however critical if you have a medical concern or any warning issues with your voice or throat area to see your GP as soon as possible. They can advise you or can refer you to the ear, nose and throat specialists if appropriate. The tips below are **not** professional medical advice but merely tried and tested strategies that successful teachers of my acquaintance swear by.

Voice care

Sip water regularly – don't gulp. Little and often is most effective for keeping the voice hydrated and this is key. If you are like me, you will love (and need!) your coffee – but like many hot drinks, it isn't actually great for the voice and can be very drying – water is always best. If you can't give up on the coffee (I can't!) just make sure you have water available to sip frequently too.

Try and avoid dusty places; this is of course tricky when teaching in some classrooms! And if there is unavoidable dust try and ventilate the room. At home a bowl of steamy hot water can help hydrate a room. Or try going for a steam room session in the evening at the gym – I have found these helpful in opening up my chest and helping preserve my voice.

Warm up your voice

If you were about to run a marathon you would first warm up, wouldn't you? Otherwise, you'd expect a pulled muscle if not another serious injury. An actor, (who also worked as a supply teacher when he was 'resting' between jobs) told me that teaching a full day was so much harder on the voice than acting in a play – even though when acting you would be speaking to a much larger audience in a huge theatre. When acting in a play – audiences are mostly very quiet (if not silent) – so it is much easier to project and let your voice fill the space. When you are teaching, sometimes it can feel like you are competing against the pupils to be heard over them and you can strain your voice. Of course, one should not try and battle by speaking over pupils – but warming up your voice before lessons is a good way of making it as effective as possible and reducing strain. There are a great number of online exercises you can do. Have a look on YouTube. Experiment and find ones that you find effective and enjoy doing – but two simple ones that were shared with me by a professional actor are the following:

Speak on a sigh or speak on a yawn

These are very simple vocal exercises but they are very effective. And as they suggest, speaking on a sigh simply means saying everything on a long, relaxed *sighhh*. It's a great exercise to do on the morning commute before you start teaching. I've done this whilst walking through the tube corridors in London on my way to give a talk!

Speaking on a sigh or speaking on a yawn helps create more space in your mouth, which is vital for avoiding vocal strain. By keeping your speech open and physically spacious really warms you up. You also avoid that awful moment when you open your mouth in front of your class to find that it has gone completely dry and you just start croaking, or your voice is squeaky high (something that doesn't command respect!). Warming up your voice can really help you communicate with confidence and, importantly, protect our greatest teaching asset.

Dealing with tension

When we feel stressed, our shoulders, neck and mouth area can feel quite tense. Doing some stretches between or before lessons can help relax the muscles. If you have too much tension, then this can really inhibit the quality and effectiveness of your voice. We often breathe shallowly when we feel tense, and this really doesn't help. Breathing deeply is important. To use your voice most effectively we need to be aware of our bodies – but we need to try and adopt a more relaxed posture and approach. Be aware of your posture and how you stand when you are talking. It can be tricky, (because of course we don't always feel comfortable and relaxed when we are teaching certain classes/topics), but trying to reduce the tension you might feel in your body will really help your voice resonate and it won't sound strained.

> ### Real life cameo
>
> When I was learning to teach – I was often told I needed to 'find the lower register' regarding my voice. I don't think it helped – because my mentor never told me how to do this. I'm sure we all prefer to listen to a deeper sounding voice as it sounds calm and purposeful. But finding that lower pitch can be challenging. Importantly, avoiding using a high pitch gives us less stress and strain. It sounds confident and purposeful. One of the key ways to do this – and it's easier said than done – is to relax. When we feel stressed, tight and taut with our shoulders up by our ears we communicate this tension through our voices. We need to have good posture to help us project our voices. If we hunch up and 'fold up' then we can't breathe as easily. We need to have a relaxed posture to feel and speak through our entire body. An actor revealed when we project we should try and 'resonate with the entire body – through to our feet which should be placed firmly so as to ground us.' He also recommended a slight bend to the knees – but what is most important, is to be relaxed and remove tension from the body so that our voice resonates freely.

Remember, when we are projecting, we should really be resonating with the whole body. Sound isn't just projected through using our mouths, instead we are like a tuning fork resonating and feeling this projection even through our feet! It sounds strange – but really think about your feet and send sound through the floor. Watch opera singers for inspiration as to how they use their whole body.

Gaining and maintaining attention without shouting

We have mentioned the importance of not raising our voice all the while because this increases the general noise level of the classroom, and it can sound like you are losing control. Grabbing pupils' attention quickly is important for managing effective behaviour. The following are strategies that I have seen are used to good effect. It's important to think about which ones might work for you – don't try everything at once because it will be too confusing for pupils and you need to use them consistently. Consistency in your behaviour is key in communicating your credibility. It is gaining this credibility that will get the class behaving as you want them to. Think about adopting some of the following ideas. Some of these we've mentioned in earlier chapters, so they may already be familiar to you:

- Choose a **specific spot** in the classroom where you always stand to give key instructions. Pupils, like puppies, need training by repetition and visual cues!
- Use a **non-verbal signal** to attract attention, for example raise one arm in the air and stand still. When pupils see this signal, they should stop talking, stand still and also hold up their arm. This way the whole class understands that the teacher wants them to be quiet and listen for instruction – without you having to say a thing.
- **Use a bell** to signal that the class should pause, be quiet and be ready to change activity. 'Hotel reception' style bells can be picked up cheaply in a variety of homeware and hardware shops. The key to using them effectively is to ding the bell smoothly and calmly, not frenetically! It's all about the poise and control of the teacher. I have seen them used effectively when the teacher is signalling moving from one task to another.
- **Count down** to create a sense of urgency for the pupils. This is ideal when you are trying to bring an activity to a close, and they have been busily participating and talking to each other about a task or question. For example, you start speaking more loudly and lower the volume as you progress, '*Five, Four, Three, two, one..*' By counting down, pupils have a moment to finish what they are saying and pay attention to you. I find that the class are often completely quiet by the time I get to three. It is much more powerful than the 'shhhing' which I sometimes hear teachers do, sounding like an out-of-control steam train is never a good move and certainly does not show authority! It is important to count *downwards* rather than upwards because you are trying to create a sense of urgency, rather than giving them freedom to carry on talking.

Vocal choices and positive non-verbal cues = pupil compliance

The use of your voice with non-verbal cues is very powerful; if they work together well they each reinforce and strengthen your message. For example, saying *'thank you'* to attract the class's attention, widening and opening your arms (to draw them in), and then giving your instructions. Saying 'thank you', loudly and with a clear downwards inflection is polite and can really grab the classes attention and show that you are in control. Combined with the wide-open arms, palms upwards to draw them in communicates that you are expecting them to listen, and that you have something positive and interesting to communicate. It is important not to speak with a rising intonation at the end of your sentence though. You are saying 'thank you' as an assertive statement expecting compliance. A rising intonation suggests that you are asking them rather than telling them. This might be appropriate when you are genuinely asking a question and you are open to their response: e.g. *'When was the Battle of Marston Moor?'* Or *'Can you explain why the answer is 0.78?'* but it is best not used when you are trying to assert authority as it shows a lack of confidence rather than authority. Some accents do mean that managing the downwards inflection is not possible, for example, I notice that Australians usually speak with an upwards inflection at the end of sentences – even when they are not posing questions.

> ### Interesting nugget
>
> Voice director Cicely Berry wrote about pitch in her book: *Your Voice and How to Use It*. She noted that a voice can becomes monotonous and lifeless if it stays on the same pitch. It doesn't entice us, but can instead sound irritating. If a voice is too loud, it can feel as though we are being talked 'at' rather than 'to', which sometimes leads to an unconscious aversion in our minds (Berry, 1994).
>
> It's a useful reminder to moderate our tone and also be aware of the effect being overly loud can have.

Check in with yourself and your voice

It is important to check in with yourself during the lesson. Be aware of any physical tension you are holding and how you might be transmitting it through your voice. It is crucial to maintain a professional front. Looking like you are in control is so essential in managing behaviour that's why letting the facade crack is not a good idea. Of course, occasionally you might want to inject urgency or another emotion into your voice for a deliberate effect (for example: encouraging the class to 'get going' tidying up after a practical lesson) and that's fine but revealing your emotions when you don't really want to isn't a good idea.

Take a pause in the lesson just to be aware of how you are feeling and sounding. If I need to re-centre myself midway through the lesson I give myself this opportunity by giving the class something purposeful to do for a couple of minutes. For example, *'in pairs, think about five reasons why Henry was successful in the first three years of his reign…'* This gives you breathing space to reset yourself if you need to – and of course pupils love the opportunity to have a purposeful talk with each other!

Deliberately being aware of yourself, injecting warmth into your voice and controlling the tone is important. This is because emotions are contagious and you can influence the emotions of those around you so that they are interested and engaged with the lesson, and know that you mean business (in a firm and friendly way, of course!)

Managing pupils' voices and responses

We have already seen that trying to get pupils to be quiet for extended periods of time isn't a winner. It's like trying to stop a pot on the stove from boiling over without adjusting the heat. However, it's worth thinking about some methods for dealing with the perennial problem of pupils shouting out the answers in class, and these are considered below.

The problem: pupils shouting out the answers. Firstly, remind them of the rules of the classroom relating to this area. Be aware that if you accept answers that are shouted out then you are prolonging the problem by rewarding such a behaviour. Consider:

- No hands up, instead you direct the question – this stops excitable children 'bursting' to tell you the answers.
- Use the phrase: *'It's a shame that I can't take really good answers if people are calling out…'*
- Remind pupils of the agreed lesson rules – again! Using 'turn and talk partners' more so that all pupils get a chance to speak.
- Give pupils a set number of talk tokens (cards or sticky notes). Each time they contribute, they hand one in. This is a good strategy to get more pupils participating and limit the over-talkers.
- Use mini-whiteboards to encourage everyone to think about the question, record a response and show it in a controlled non-verbal way. You can then select a person to explain their answer.

- If pupils persistently call out, speak with them after the class. Acknowledge their enthusiasm, but explain that you can't accept their answers when they choose to call out. If they persist then (with regret) you will have to follow the school's behaviour system and sanction it.
- When pupils are reluctant to participate, quietly encourage them or have a few words with them when you circulate the class. Sometimes it can be a good idea to key them in that you will be asking them to contribute in a few minutes so that they have thinking time. Setting a supportive classroom culture is key in encouraging them to want to participate.

Giving instructions

A confident teacher who manages behaviour well communicates clearly and with certainty. The clarity of our instructions is so important. If we ramble or we are unclear then we risk confusing pupils. The following are some strategies to think about if behaviour is sometimes derailed by pupils saying – *'we don't know what we are doing,'* or alternatively, if they happily go off and complete the entirely wrong thing! If you ever had the experience of thinking that you have communicated clearly but then after they have set off realising that they don't know what they should be doing and having to pull them all back (with all the tricky behaviour issues that causes), then these tips are for you:

- We can't pre-plan *all* our instructions as we need to be flexible and adapt to the changing circumstances in our lesson – however, planning key phrases in advance can improve clarity and confidence. Write them on your lesson plan or on a sticky note so that you can easily see them. This often means that you have planned and foreseen any pitfalls in what you are asking them to do therefore it is much more successful.
- Don't overwhelm pupils – less is more. Sometimes as an observer I've listened to overwhelming or very complex multi-part instructions. Instead of giving too many stages – get the class clearly focused on what they should be doing first.
- Keep sentences clear, crisp and short.
- Try and stick to four words, for example: *'Pens down and listening!'*

- Think about reinforcing the verbal instructions with the instructions also shown on the board so that the class can easily refer back to them.
- Check that pupils properly understand what you have asked them to do. For example, selecting one pupil to remind the class what exactly they must do. If they do this accurately then that's great – and the class as a whole have had a reminder. If they misremember or have got it wrong it gives you a chance to correct any misunderstandings.
- Mini-whiteboards can provide useful checks and help pupils see what order they need to tackle tasks in. Writing down the order in which they need to do things on the board make a useful visual reminder. Likewise, mini-whiteboards can be used for sentence starters or other strategies used to help pupils who feel 'stuck' getting started.

Word up

Great teachers are skilled with the words they choose to use, and they are acutely aware of their impact. For example, they use words that motivate and are careful about what information they choose to mention and what they omit. They explain what they **do** want to see, rather than what they **don't** in terms of behaviour. For example, if I tell you that I don't want you to think about a giant green pug with a baseball hat skate boarding, I bet that's exactly what you are thinking about!

Great teachers talk about what behaviour they *do* want to see instead, so if, for example they see a group of pupils within the class who have not got their textbooks out yet, they might tactically ignore this for a moment. They first highlight the pupils who have got themselves organised and are ready to start the lesson: *'Well done, I can see people have got their books out and open to page 64'.* This encourages those who are late to start complying with the request. It also creates a sense of urgency as it implies that everyone else is ready to start the lesson. It is much more effective than saying: *'Seamus, Marta and Henri get your books out'*, which makes the children who have been singled out feel picked on. This can also fuel resentment which might result in deliberate sighing and eye rolling as they get their books out. Great teachers highlight the behaviour that they expect to see and choose their words carefully to keep motivation high. Words, and the way we use them, really matter.

Don't say	Because the pupil hears	Instead try	Effect on pupil
'This is really easy.'	I don't need to try (it's easy) – or if they get stuck: I must be really stupid because the teacher has said it is easy.	*'You are ready for this. You might make mistakes and that's fine because you are learning. Let's recap what you need to do.'*	Clarity about task and permission to make mistakes.
'Do you have any questions?'	Really it should be clear. I don't want to put my head above the parapet even though I might be confused.	*'What questions do you have?'*	Great. I can seek clarification, it is expected. I won't feel foolish asking questions.
'Put your phone away, Omar…'	I feel picked on and singled out. This teacher does not like me.	*'Right, I can see everyone is ready to start,'* looking meaningfully at Omar and giving a pause before saying: *'Omar, Ryan, would you like to put your phones away or should I keep them for you?'*	I better put my phone away before I get called out. The teacher has spotted me, but she's given me a choice of how to react so I keep my self-esteem.

What's your speed?

Think about a recent meeting that you attended that didn't particularly interest you. The person running it was keen to communicate something that was new to you, and they spoke very quickly. Perhaps you persevered, perhaps you switched off and thought about what you would cook for dinner. Imagine after about 30 minutes of this meeting you were asked to individually complete a piece of work about this topic – how would you feel? How might you react if you felt anxious about this? How might your behaviour alter?

Sometimes when I'm observing lessons, I'm astounded by the pace at which teachers talk. This is particularly the case in secondary, where a teacher might have taught a particular lesson multiple times to various classes. The familiarity that the teacher feels with the subject material means that they often forget that it's new, or not securely understood by the pupils. They might be using new or challenging vocabulary without giving time to check for understanding. The danger with speaking far too quickly is clear. If we lose pupils, or if they feel overwhelmed or anxious about the speed of information then they might get distracted, overwhelmed or disheartened. All of which can lead to off-task or difficult behaviour – after all, if we don't understand, think we are going to fail or look foolish in front of our peers then acting out is a great way to disguise this. Another reason for our speedy pace is our nerves. When we feel nervous we speak too quickly, and pupils pick up on our nervousness and they lose confidence in us. Using an appropriate speed of voice, and adapting this to the class, as well as adding appropriate emphasis and interest to our voice is a way of maintaining control, establishing credibility and helping better learning.

Try this out

Read the following extract – first in your head – to become familiar with the content. Then read it aloud, and either time yourself or ask a friend to time you. The content of the extract doesn't matter, but as I often walk in the mountains of Colorado on holiday, I thought I'd give you something that might be interesting and potentially life-saving. Here's a few tips about what to do if you meet some dangerous wild animals, in this instance a bear!

There are many wild animals living in Colorado – and most wild animals can be dangerous when they are confronted. They key term here is the word 'wild'. Some of the most dangerous animals in Colorado include bears – and don't think you can outrun these guys. They are fast! Make sure you don't leave any food outside, and keep your dustbins in the garage to deter unwelcome visitors. When hiking, ensure you make plenty of noise as many animals will actively avoid being caught in a human's path. If you do come across a bear – don't turn and run as it will activate their prey instinct. Instead, try and make yourself look as large as possible, stand your ground, speak in a firm calm voice and slowly back away giving the bear space to leave. Never stand between a bear and its cubs. Avoid direct eye contact as it can be seen as aggressive. Bear spray is something that hikers often take with them. Keep it ready, but don't use it unless the bear rushes you and is within 30 feet. If you do get into a violent confrontation with a bear in Colorado do not play dead, instead aim for the face and snout of the bear. But the main thing to do is to try and avoid being in the position of facing a bear in the first place!

If you recorded yourself, listen to it before answering the questions below. The pace of speech is important. Pace is defined as the speed at which someone delivers their words. It can be fast, slow or moderate, and can change throughout a speech. The best teachers alter their pace depending on the reaction of the class. They also use emphasis to highlight key messages, important words and essential information.

- How long did it take you to read it?
- How much can you remember of the content?
- Do you think you were too fast, too slow or just right? Do you think your pupils would think the same?
- How does the average timing of words per minute compare for you?

> **Interesting nugget**
>
> Research indicates that speaking time in normal conversation is between 110-150 words per minute, but this can often feel very fast if we are expecting pupils to understand new material! This is particularly true if pupils are expected to make notes, or if they have lower levels of literacy.
>
> Make sure if you are teaching pupils with English as an Additional Language that you don't rush and ensure that you clarify key vocabulary. Also bear in mind students that are neurodivergent. Some pupils will also have difficulty processing information and when we speak very quickly this can really cause issues.
>
> When we feel stressed or emotional, our pace of speech can speed up which does not help. So, remember to make an effort to pace carefully and pause as you go.

Have another go at reading it aloud. Before you do so think about your timing. Are there bits that you think would benefit from a pause, slowing down, or speeding up? Varying the pace keeps pupils interested and allows you to direct them to the most important parts. Think about where you might want to add emphasis. Record yourself and then share your recording with a friend or colleague.

- How long did you take this time?
- Do you think you sounded better?
- What effect did any changes have on the listeners' comprehension?
- Do you have any vocal habits or mannerisms that could throw off the listener?

Getting feedback from a trusted friend or colleague can be so useful in helping you really use your voice to help keep pupils focused, interested and well managed. They can highlight things you may not even be aware of, for example, you might have a distracting habit of saying a specific phrase that you didn't know about. Once, during training in a school, somebody gently pointed out on an evaluation form that it might be helpful for me to know, that I repeatedly use the phrase: *'if you can see what I mean?'*. Don't be too hard on yourself, and if you use frequent fillers (erm, umm) although these can break up the flow of what you are saying and can suggest nervousness, some do allow your class time to process what you are saying.

Pause for thought

Finally, although using our voice effectively is key in being brilliant at behaviour management – we mustn't forget the effect of a pause. It can create an impressive dramatic effect, giving pupils time to amend their behaviour as they realise that you've spotted them. It can also allow pupils time to process what you have said and re-engages them.

Ultimately silence can be so powerful. Standing still saying nothing stops you saying something that might inflame the situation. Many people rush to fill up the silence because it can feel uncomfortable – staying silent shows composure, confidence and control – it shows calm, authority and gravitas.

Way forward

After reading this chapter you will have received ideas about how your voice can influence behaviour. You might have decided that there are some strategies you would like to trial out because you think that they will be useful. You might like to observe another member of staff to see how they use their voice effectively. Or you might like to ask a colleague or friend to give you some feedback about the use of your voice and how you moderate noise levels in your lessons.

Areas that I think are working well with my classes/individuals are:

_____
_____
_____
_____
_____
_____

Areas I would like to work on relating to voice control:

1 _____

2 _____

3 _____

The planned actions I am going to take are:

1 _____

2 _____

3 _____

Review: How did it go? What did I learn? What are my reflections? Am I going to keep any new strategies? Do I have any further steps?

_____

_____

_____

_____

_____

_____

_____

_____

_____

_____

_____

_____

_____

_____

8 You are not alone: engaging with others

This book has shared many practical ways in which you, as the class teacher, can behaviour proof your teaching. But it is important to remember that you are not alone. A pupil's or class's behaviour doesn't exist within a vacuum. They are part of a whole educational community which is overseen by the Headteacher or Principal. It is likely that you might have some additional adults in lessons too – teaching assistants or progress mentors. While their role is clearly predominantly to help ensure the educational progress of pupils, they are often a welcome second set of eyes and can provide valuable feedback, and sometimes useful support or insight to behaviour. Of course, sometimes they too also require support and guidance regarding behaviour themselves.

Last, but certainly not least, parents and carers have the pivotal role and responsibility in influencing young people's behaviour. Especially as in most cases, children are at home and in their charge for much longer than they are at school! Of course, in some instances dealing with tricky responses from parents and carers can be another, if not the biggest, 'behavioural' challenge in itself! In this chapter we will briefly look at some strategies for these areas and suggest some approaches and ideas for you to consider when having conversations with parents. But remember the key thing: you are not alone. While there is a huge amount that that you can personally do to influence behaviour of your pupils, there are others who can help and provide support and who have the ultimate responsibility.

Goal: interacting effectively with other adults

As we have unpicked in the previous chapters managing behaviour has a range of components to it. As you have read each chapter you will have reflected on which areas are working well for you, and where you might like to put some further focus. Our goal now should be to think about our interactions and approaches with the other adults who we have contact with, considering how these can help us towards our goal of being brilliant at behaviour management.

Within the classroom

If you are lucky enough to have another adult working alongside you in the classroom, then they can help you instil better behaviour. In many lessons I have visited, the teaching assistant (or other adult) has positively influenced behaviour by being a good role model, emulating the manners and responses we want to see in our pupils. Having another adult in the room gives you the opportunity to role play responses to questions and activities and set high standards of behaviour. Effective feedback between you and your teaching assistant enables you to receive useful insights about the behaviour, attitudes and understanding of your learners. There might be things that you were completely unaware of (after all it can be hard to get a read on how all 30 pupils are responding at once!).

Asking your teaching assistant to focus in on how some specific pupils are responding can give you valuable feedback. We have seen in previous chapters when pupils don't understand, feel frustrated or incompetent then this is when tricky behaviour starts to emerge. It is easy to disrupt the lesson and look cool rather than feel like someone who 'can't' complete the work or understand the learning. A great teaching assistant is a massive asset to embedding great behaviour for learning because they can help detect where there might be challenges for pupils. Think carefully about how your teaching assistant is deployed and the purpose that they have in your lesson. But also, be flexible, sometimes it will be appropriate to change and alter who they are working with.

Real life cameo

Insights from your teaching assistant

A friend who teaches in a Year 3 and 4 mixed class told me about a challenge she had been having with a new pupil. He had been 'moved' from another local primary school. The information she had received about him suggested that he would continue with his defiant and very difficult behaviour. Initially, she said the situation was very stressful. He behaved in a loud way, refusing to follow instructions, often doing the complete opposite!

My friend found it increasingly challenging, and he was repeatedly told off with SLT often called to offer support. The most recent time I saw her she said things had improved 100 per cent partly due to an observation by her teaching assistant. He had noticed that the pupil seemed to be desperately craving attention, and whenever he received the slightest bit of positive interaction his behaviour improved. My friend admitted that this was the piece of advice that helped her achieve massive improvements in his behaviour. She admitted, it didn't feel natural to try and immediately find a positive and to 'catch him being good'. However now his behaviour has vastly improved. All through being open to constructive feedback from her perceptive teaching assistant.

Senior leaders hold the overview of behaviour management and they have the status and experience to do this. It is important that there is an effective overall behavioural management policy for all school staff to follow. This gives class teachers clarity and confidence in what they are doing, and they can feel supported that their actions are underpinned by a helpful behaviour management system.

The goal should be to have productive and professional communications with them on a two-way basis. Senior leaders need to be alerted to any areas that class teachers are finding tricky, or aspects of the school behaviour management system that would benefit from further support, guidance or clarity. Senior leaders need to have a good overview about the effectiveness of the behaviour policy from teachers who are dealing with it lesson after lesson and day after day. Is it effective? Is it user-friendly? Is it leading to improved behaviour for learning? It should be the case that you are able to ask for support, guidance and clarity to help you best maximise the behaviour in your lessons. It is important therefore that senior leaders are approachable and maintain curiosity, rather than judgement when things are difficult in lessons. *'What are the areas that staff are finding hard, and what can we do to support them to improve behaviour for learning?'* – is a better approach than attributing blame when staff find things tricky.

Senior leaders in secondary schools and colleges also have the birds' eye view of a student's behaviour in different areas of the school. If a student's behaviour is being problematic in *most* of the lessons across the school, then a different approach will be needed as opposed when they are acting out in just one lesson. A joined-up approach across the school really matters. None of us are 'finished' with our learning, and different staff will have different skills and competencies relating to behaviour management. The senior leaders are in a position where they can use this overview, utilising various staff's different skills – enabling everyone to improve their behaviour for learning teaching. Whether it is through sharing CPD, looking at new behaviour strategies, links with relevant agencies or developing specific interventions with individual pupils or groups of pupils.

Parents and carers

Developing an effective partnership with parents and carers – and having the confidence and skill to discuss children's behaviour and what can be done to improve it is a vital part of any school or college's approach to improving behaviour for learning. The goal is that staff are confident, supported and clear on how to do this. Schools will have a clearly written Home School Agreement which explains the values, policies and procedures, but it is how it is implemented and how relationships are fostered between school and home which is the bedrock of better behaviour for learning.

Reality: reflecting on relationships

There are three main groups of other adults that we work with to improve behaviour for learning. Senior teachers and parents and carers clearly have a critical lead role here. For some teachers, teaching assistants, learning mentors and other adults will have a supportive influence in helping with behaviour, although in most cases this is not likely to be their main role.

Key questions to think about with senior leaders and other staff

1. Are you clear about the behaviour management policy in your setting?
2. Do you feel that you implement it appropriately? Do you feel that you can ask for guidance about aspects of it?
3. Do you feel that you can ask for support/CPD/advice for behaviour management without negative judgement?
4. Do you have a trusted colleague, line manager or mentor who you can share concerns with and gain practical support with behaviour for learning?
5. Do you know where in the setting there are practitioners who have expertise in particular areas – that you might like to develop – for example: non-verbal communication, dealing with disruption or planning lessons for engagement and quality learning?
6. Do you use the school/college reward and sanctions? Do you find that these are effective?
7. If you are having specific challenges with a pupil or a group of pupils' behaviour, do senior leaders help you to develop solutions and effective strategies to improve things?

8   Do you receive constructive feedback on behaviour for learning in lesson observations?

9   If you feel that if you need to 'reset' things with a class, or if you decide that you need to make major changes to the way that you do things to re-establish your authority, do you have a colleague or senior leader you can ask for advice or support whilst you do this?

10 Do you make effective use of any SEND information about your pupils? And do you ask for advice from the SENCO about how to implement this?

11 Are you open to feedback from any relevant staff and adults?

12 Do you evaluate how you work with other adults in lessons to review what is working well and what could be improved?

13 Do you share your intentions and plans regarding behaviour for learning so that other staff (in your lessons) are appropriately briefed?

Key questions to think about with parents and carers

1   Are you clear about the protocols for contacting a pupil's home?

2   When you notice things aren't going as well as they should be with an individual's learning and behaviour do you get in contact with parents promptly?

3   Do you try and suggest solutions and tackle conversations with a positive mindset? Do you look for common ground?

4   Are parents and carers sufficiently well informed about any strategies and approaches you are taking so that they can reinforce them during behaviour at home? For example, completing homework, looking at the targets on the daily report card, etc.

5   Do you take opportunities to pass on the positive behaviours you have noticed with parents and carers regarding their child?

6   Do you always take care to make sure that you are informed about the child's SEND needs and any other concerns that the school might be aware of?

7   Are you good at checking in and keeping parents informed and updated? Of course, you are likely not to be able to solve things immediately but following up and through are so important.

8   Do you feel that you have good communication skills when you are contacting parents and carers?

Opportunities: communicating with your colleagues

There are of course, countless opportunities to improve and learn from the other adults in the school and home to help improve behaviour for learning. It would be exhausting and counterproductive to try and do everything! It is important to think about what the areas of concern you have are – and then how best to work on them. Although they are likely to be quite individual to you – it is also true that there are probably other teachers in the same boat. Sharing the concerns are the first steps to finding solutions.

It is for that reason why **communication** is the most important thing. Whether there are challenges across a whole class, or you are finding a few individuals' behaviour tricky, communicating and sharing your concerns with the most relevant other is the first step. This might be a pastoral lead, line manager or Head of Department, or even the senior leader/Headteacher. Trying to conceal difficulties is only storing up bigger problems along the way as difficult behaviour becomes entrenched and harder to change. As someone who had some responsibility for behaviour management – I never minded if somebody asked for advice or support – but especially when they explained what they had already tried first. Having a positive and honest conversations with somebody who can advise and support you to make changes is always the first step. The same is true for communication with parents and carers, don't leave it – gather information and if it is your place to do so – make the contact.

Empowering not undermining

Although it might feel like a great solution to transfer all of the difficult pupils to a colleague, this approach can be counterproductive. On occasion, it might be appropriate to remove a pupil from a behaviourally inflammable situation – and knowing where there is a teacher buddy who has a class nearby that can occasionally facilitate this can be useful. However, if pupils are regularly being taken to other classes, or if senior leaders repeatedly need to stay in the lesson to instil calm, then it is ultimately undermining for the class teacher. Instead, ask for specific advice about how to handle a particular pupil or by taking the opportunity to observe them being taught by a different teacher might provide a more useful long-term insight. If you are planning to reset the attitude of the class by, for example, re-organising the class seating plan, then asking the senior teacher or line manager to pop in briefly (on a pretext, such as: *'I'm just collecting some dictionaries'*) might be a good way to bolster your confidence regarding your actions without feeling undermined. You will feel much more confident to deal with the class and to re-organise the seating – because you know that some casual support will be on hand if it is needed.

> ### Real life cameo
>
> A secondary school teacher told me that he was experiencing behavioural problems in his lessons. He had recently moved from a school with a very punitive behaviour policy – and his overly severe approach at his new school was causing conflict with several children. He sought out the school SENCO who gave him specific advice about how to effectively manage these pupils individually so they would remain focused and motivated in lessons without constant reprimands (which were the source of conflict). These included various practical adjustments, such as, letting them use a small fidget toy, when they were struggling to sit still when class reading was happening. Using the pupil's name much more, so that they knew they were expected to respond to questions and they were cued into when they were expected to respond. Specific advice regarding another pupil focused on breaking down the learning task into much smaller sections, and seating them at the front of the classroom where the teacher could check in with them more easily, rather than singling them out in front of everyone. These small but important adjustments helped manage their behaviour better and meant that they re-engaged with the learning. The teacher was then also able to give meaningful praise: behaviour and learning was much improved.

There are lots of useful reminders about working with parents and carers to improve behaviour – and that could be a book in its own right. Conversations about behaviour are more productive with parents and carers if:

- You are the correct person to make contact.
- You ensure that you speaking to the right person – have you got their name and title absolutely right?
- You have accurate information about the situation.

- You listen carefully…first. There is always the tendency to jump in, but it can calm the situation to let them 'let it all out first'.
- You make contact when you are emotionally calm yourself – otherwise the situation will be inflamed. This is critical.

If there's a behaviour issue or a serious incident – be descriptive rather than apportioning blame first. Describe what the situation was and what happened – rather than making judgements. Take the emotion out of the situation. Further reminders to help with parent/carer conversations:

- Plan for the meeting and think about what you want to achieve. Make sure that you have all relevant information before the meeting.
- Be aware that the child might exhibit very different behaviour at home.
- Know that the parent/carer will be aware of things that you will have no idea about – so give them the opportunity to tell you. Sometimes the child might be experiencing significant challenges in their home life which could impact their behaviour, for example a family divorce, redundancy, death or severe illness of a close family member.
- For some parents/carers criticism of their child can feel very personal, like it is criticism of them. Some parents and carers are under huge amounts of stress and don't know what to do to improve things and that might mean that they respond with hostility.
- On occasion, the pupils' behaviour is a direct reaction to the parents/carers' actions. Sometimes you might start to think that there might be possible potential safeguarding issues. If you start to feel this – then ensure that you immediately contact the safeguarding lead in the school. Do not investigate it yourself – pass on your concerns to the safeguarding lead right away. Make this the top priority before anything else.

When communicating with parents/carers

- Remember you are after the same outcome – improved behaviour and attitudes to learning for the child. Keep this common goal in mind and refer to it.
- Think carefully about your choice of medium: email, telephone or face-to-face. It is often much better to have a face-to-face conversation because there's nuance in non-verbal communication that can help

de-escalate a situation. Emails can be misconstrued on occasion. However, consider if you might want another staff member present to support you. Plan for this in advance.

- Always follow up, especially if a parent/carer has contacted you first and you are not prepared because it is unexpected. You might not have the answer right away but you can leave a holding message telling them when it will be looked at. Ensure that everybody understands any follow up actions.

- Think about the layout of the room when having meetings. Sitting parents/carers across from you with a table between you can appear more much more formal and confrontational than having them sit near or alongside you.

- If you ask them to take a seat and give them a choice of seats – this can make the situations appear less threatening for them as you are offering them a choice.

- Avoid starting with: *'How are you?'* as an initial greeting. They are not likely to be very pleased with coming into school/college, or they might feel stressed or very concerned or upset. It is much better to start with: *'Thank you for coming in today'*. This keeps it positive, but professional.

- Try and communicate that you are trying to get the best resolution and that you care about the child's well-being and learning. Even if you are having to communicate a message that will not be appreciated or received well – you can give that communication in humane way. Ensure that there is clarity about the next step regarding the child's behaviour whatever that might be.

- Remember difficult conversations only become easier the more you have them. If you find them very daunting think about things that might help. For example: further training, observing others who are more experienced or practising tricky conversations beforehand with your line manager.

- Finally, remember there will be someone more senior who can have the conversation with you, or on your behalf.

- Don't forget to keep parents and carers informed and follow up. Ensure that any positive changes are communicated too. Developing ongoing constructive relationships with parents and carers is a critical way of ensuring long term improvements with pupil behaviour.

Real life cameo

The difference between sympathy and empathy

A school counsellor once gave me a useful piece of advice – when I was finding it hard to talk to parents/carers. She told me to think carefully about the attitude I was displaying and reminded me that there was a difference between sympathy and empathy. When we are sympathetic to someone we feel sorry for them – it's very *'poor you – that's terrible for you.'* Whilst some people might like this – it can be construed as patronising (especially from a teacher), but importantly it leaves them dwelling on their issues without any progress. Of course, when we are dealing with behaviour management parents might be having a very tough time for numerous reasons, and it is important to acknowledge that. However, we need to not just leave them in that situation feeling hopeless. Empathy is showing more understanding for their situation. However, we won't have personally exactly experienced the same situation, and even if we have each person will have a unique perspective. This is why the counsellor suggested saying: *'I appreciate that might be difficult/hard/challenging',* rather than *'I understand, or I know how you feel.'* Sometimes saying *'I know how you feel'* and making presumptions about how someone else is feeling in a difficult time can result in really inflaming the situation whereas *'I appreciate'* is a better, more considered approach and is likely to lead to a better resolution.

Way forward

After reading this chapter you will have received some food for thought about the role of other adults in assisting you to manage behaviour effectively.

Reflect on your relationships and interactions with senior leaders, parents, carers and other staff.

_____

_____

_____

Aspects I believe I'm successful at when working with other adults to raise standards of behaviour:

1 _____

2 _____

3 _____

Areas I would like to work on relating to wider staff and pastoral relationships:

1 _____

2 _____

3 _____

Review: How did it go? What did I learn? What are my reflections? Do I have any further steps? Do I need to seek support/advice from elsewhere?

_____
_____
_____
_____
_____
_____
_____
_____
_____
_____
_____
_____
_____

You are not alone

Finally, remember that we are all still learning. The great thing about teaching is that every day is a fresh start with your pupils. There will be many opportunities for you to trial ideas in this book, to share them and to develop your own effective insights about what works for you and your pupils. Thank you so much for reading this book. I wish you all the very best with your teaching, your pupils and your mission to Be Brilliant at Behaviour Management.

With all best wishes,

Caroline Bentley-Davies @realcbd

www.bentley-davies.co.uk

Bibliography

Asch, S. E., 1951. *Effects of group pressure upon the modification and distortion of judgments*. In: H. Guetzkow (ed.) *Groups, Leadership and Men*. Pittsburgh: Carnegie Press. pp. 222–236.

Berry, C., 1994. *Your Voice and How to Use It*. London: Virgin.

Brue Hood, P., 2024. *The Science of Happiness: Seven Lessons for Living Well*. Simon & Schuster.

Cambridge University Press, 2025. *Tone*. In: *Cambridge English Dictionary*. Available at: https://dictionary.cambridge.org/dictionary/english/tone [Accessed 26 October 2025].

Cialdini, R. B., Reno, R. R., & Kallgren, C. A. (1990). A focus theory of normative conduct: Recycling the concept of norms to reduce littering in public places. *Journal of Personality and Social Psychology*, 58(6), 1015–1026.

Clear, J. (2018). *Atomic Habits: An easy & proven way to build good habits & break bad ones*. London: Penguin Random House.

Csikszentmihalyi, M. (1975). *Beyond boredom and anxiety: Experiencing flow in work and play*. San Francisco: Jossey-Bass.

Cuddy, A.J.C., 2012. *Your body language may shape who you are* [video online]. TED. Available at: https://www.youtube.com/watch?v=Ks-_Mh1QhMc [Accessed 25 October 2025].

Dwyer, C., 2006. *Using Praise to Enhance Student Resilience and Learning Outcomes*. Educational Testing Service. Available at: https://www.apa.org/education-career/k12/using-praise [Accessed 26 October 2025].

Flora, S.R., 2000. Praise's magic reinforcement ratio: Five to one gets the job done. *The Behavior Analyst Today*, 1(4), pp.64–69. Available at: https://www.researchgate.net/publication/276078120_Praise%27s_magic_reinforcement_ratio_Five_to_one_gets_the_job_done [Accessed 26 October 2025].

Ginott, H.G., 1972. *Teacher and Child: A Book for Parents and Teachers*. New York: Macmillan. p. 15.

Mark, G., 2023. 'We started studying attention span length over 20 years ago...', *CBS News*, 15 October. Available at: https://www.cbsnews.com/news/are-attention-spans-getting-shorter-and-does-it-matter/ [Accessed 26 October 2025].

McAleer, P., Mahrholz, G., & Belin, P. (2017). *The sound of trustworthiness: Acoustic-based modulation of perceived voice personality*. *PLOS ONE*, 12(10), e0185651. https://doi.org/10.1371/journal.pone.0185651

Mehrabian, A. (1971). *Silent messages*. Belmont, CA: Wadsworth.

North, A. C. Hargreaves, D. J., & McKendrick, J. (1999). The influence of in-store music on wine selections. *Journal of Applied Psychology, 84*(2), 271–276.

Pogue, D. (2023) 'Are attention spans getting shorter (and does it matter)?', CBS News, 15 October. Available at: https://www.cbsnews.com/news/are-attention-spans-getting-shorter-and-does-it-matter/

Psychology Today (n.d.) 'Broken windows theory', Psychology Today (United Kingdom). Available at: https://www.psychologytoday.com/gb/basics/broken-windows-theory

West, M. (2025) 'Maslow's hierarchy of needs: Uses and criticism', Medical News Today, 20 June. Available at: https://www.medicalnewstoday.com/articles/maslows-hierarchy-of-needs

Whitmore, J., 1992. *Coaching for Performance: Growing Human Potential and Purpose: The Principles and Practice of Coaching and Leadership.* London: Nicholas Brealey Publishing.

Wilson, J.Q. & Kelling, G.L., 1982. *Broken Windows: The police and neighbourhood safety.* The Atlantic, 249(3), pp.29–38.

Index

Asch, Solomon 50
attention spans, decline in 84

behavioural norms 26
Berry, Cicely 117
body language 51, 55, 56–1
    confident 62–4, 66–1
    quadrant 60–2
    self-reflecting questions on 63
    see also non-verbal communication

chunking, lesson 84–5
classroom code 34–5
control, zone of 22

detentions 26, 39, 48–1
direct control 21
display strategy 24, 43, 81–2, 100

end-of-lesson routines 36–1
environmental priming 22–3
    strategies for 24–5
esteem needs 92–3

feedback 9, 86–1, 93, 128
first impressions 19–1, 26–1
flow, lesson 20, 36

gestures, non-verbal 58–1, 65–67
group behaviour, power of 50
GROW coaching approach 9–11

homework 26, 36, 48–1

influence, zone of 22

Landsberg, Max 9
lesson foundations 19–1
    direct control 21–2

environmental priming 22–5
first impressions 19–1, 26–1
pre-planned responses to student
    comments/behaviour 29–1
rapport 30–1
scripting 27–1
visualisation 28
lesson ideas 85–86
lesson planning 74–78
    chunking, lesson 84–5
    classroom environment and displays
        in, role of 81–2
    classroom maintenance and 82
    for engagement and high
        expectations 75–76
    explanations 83–5
    feedback and evaluation 87
    grouping strategy in 78–1
    high expectations, setting 80–1
    learning objective in 76–1
    lesson ideas 85–86
    Lesson Study 86
    lesson transitions, effective
        management of 85
    observation tasks and checklists 86
    self-reflection on successful 76
    for SEND accommodations 79
    using social media and online
        forums 86
Lesson Study 86
low-level disruptive behaviour 38

Mark, Gloria 84
Maslow's hierarchy of needs 90–3
    esteem needs 92–3
    physiological needs 91
    safety needs 91–2
    self-actualisation 93
    social belonging 92

needs, Maslow's hierarchy of *see* Maslow's hierarchy of needs
negative non-verbal communication 61, 62
non-verbal communication 56–1, 116
  adaptability 59
  awareness of individual differences, disabilities, and cultural factors 58–1
  brief eye contacts 51, 57–1, 69
  classroom management through 67
  de-escalation 68–1
  gestures 58–1, 65–67
  non-verbal behaviour signals 57
  palm faced down motion 67
  passive 62
  power posing and confidence 66
  as sanctions for rule-breakers 51
  teacher presence and confidence 57–1
  voice control with non-verbal cues 116–1

other adults and behaviour management 127
  parent/carer for behaviour improvement, communication with 133–5
  parents and carers 130–1
  seeking advice and support from 132–3
  senior leaders 129–1
  staff, communication with 132
  sympathy vs. empathy 136
  teaching assistants 128–1

parents and carers 130–1
parent–school partnerships 130
passive non-verbal communication 62
peer pressure 51
physiological needs 91
positive non-verbal communication 60–1, 66–1
praising 98–1
psychological safety needs 91–2

relationship-building
  active listening 100–1
  foundations for 95–103
  parents, positive communication with 100
  positive 89–1
  praising 98–1
  pupils' self-management skills, developing 103
  recognition and rewards for works 99
  self-awareness 102
  sense of belonging, creating 95–96
  showing interest and recognizing individuality 97–1
  students' work in classroom, displaying 100
  supportive classroom culture, creating 101
  trust through actions, creating 102
routines 19, 33
  clarity of 35
  end-of-lesson 36–1
  homework, setting 36
  lesson-start and transition 36
  positive 37
rule(s) 19, 33
  acknowledgement of others point of view 46
  breakers 37–1, 43
  clarity of 43
  classroom code 34–5
  consistency 33–4
  detention intervention 48–1
  enforcement strategy 45–46
  escalation for high-risk behaviours 39
  goal of 34
  improvements 41–47
  low-level disruptive behaviour, sanctions for 38
  meaning of 44–5
  non-verbal sanctions 51
  peer observation 51
  positive peer pressure 51
  rule-making authority 45

sanctions 37–1, 48–2
self-reflection on 40–1
simplicity 47
three-part script approach 46
transparency 43–4
visual display of 43

safety needs 91–2
school behaviour policy 41–2
scripting 27–1, 46
self-actualisation 93
self-esteem 92–3
self-reflection
   body language 63
   lesson planning 76
   other adults and behaviour
      management 130–1
   rules and routines 40–1
   voice control 111–13
SEND pupils
   lesson planning for 79
   non-verbal communication for 52
senior leaders 129–1
sense of belonging 90, 92, 95–96

teaching assistants 128–1
tone of voice 108–10

uniform rules 42–3

visualisation 28, 43
voice care 113
   relaxation 114
   vocal exercises 114
   vocal warm-up 114
voice control 105, 110
   classroom attention through,
      gaining 115–16
   instruction clarity through 119–1
   with non-verbal cues 116–1
   pace control 121–4
   pause and silence, importance of 124
   pupils' voices and responses,
      managing 118–1
   self-awareness, voice 117–1
   self-reflection on 111–13
   tone of voice 108–10
   word choice 120–1
voice effectiveness 106–7

Whitmore, John, Sir 9

zones
   of control and influence 22
   of non-verbal communication 60–2